Brother John has given us a great gift by updating his reflections on prayer. Writing with wit, passion, and clarity, Brother John graciously invites us into a deeper prayer life—underscoring the importance of prayer in the life of a disciple while not turning it into a duty or burden. I found the last section—dealing with specific issues in the disciple's prayer life—to be especially practical and useful.

James T. Birchfield, Senior Pastor,
First Presbyterian Church, Houston, Texas

The Golden Anniversary version of John Bisagno's classic *The Power of Positive Praying* is precisely that . . . golden! Writing a book on prayer is one thing; revising it after a fifty-year PhD in the School of Prayer is quite another. I have been deeply moved and blessed by this treasure of the kingdom.

Kirbyjon Caldwell, Senior Pastor,
Windsor Village United Methodist Church

Most of faithful Western Christianity knows that prayer is the battle. And since the Enlightenment, most of Western Christianity has *thought* more than it has prayed. Brother John Bisagno draws us back again not only to prayer but to the transforming power of prayer.

The Rt. Rev'd Clark WP Lowenfield, Bishop,
Anglican Diocese of the Western Gulf Coast

The Power of Positive Praying will help grow your trust in God as you see His mighty hand move in your life. I recommend you read this book to sharpen and deepen your life on your knees. John Bisagno is a wonderful friend to me, and we have prayed together countless times. He is the right man to teach us to pray more fervently and effectively.

Gregg Matte, Pastor, Houston's First Baptist Church
and author of *I AM Changes Who I Am*

THE
POWER
OF
POSITIVE
PRAYING

50TH

ANNIVERSARY

EDITION

THE

POWER

OF

POSITIVE

PRAYING

JOHN BISAGNO

B&H
PUBLISHING GROUP

NASHVILLE, TENNESSEE

978-1-4336-8580-4

Published by B&H Publishing Group
Nashville, Tennessee

Dewey Decimal Classification: 248.3
Subject Heading: PRAYER \ CHRISTIAN LIFE

1 2 3 4 5 6 7 • 19 18 17 16 15

To my precious wife, Uldine, who has exemplified a life of positive praying for sixty wonderful years—and more.

I love you angel,
Your John

CONTENTS

SECTION 3: **FURTHER**

Jesus' Priority in Prayer

Charles H. Gabriel expressed the desire of every believer in his beloved hymn "More like the Master." Peter taught that we can and should become precisely that.

> *For even hereunto were ye called: because Christ*
> *also suffered for us, leaving us an example, that*
> *ye should follow his steps. (1 Pet. 2:21 KJV)*

Nowhere was He more our example than in prayer.

Jesus knelt to pray (Luke 22:41). And we do the same. We kneel reverently as did Solomon in the temple. We bow before Him, as did Abraham at Bethel, Moses at Sinai, Elijah at Carmel, and Jonah at Nineveh.

Like the Master, our lives are marked by prayer. The earthly ministry of our Lord began and ended in prayer:

> *Now when all the people were baptized, it came to pass, that Jesus also being baptized, and praying, the heaven was opened. (Luke 3:21 KJV)*

> *Then said Jesus, Father forgive them; for they know not what they do. And they parted his raiment, and cast lots. (Luke 23:34 KJV)*

When we pray, Satan trembles. When we pray, heaven's gates open wide. When we pray, desperation fades and trials wither before us like grass before the scorching sun. When we pray, power comes, love fills our heart, and life is filled with song.

And there is glorious privilege in prayer. William W. Walford said it well:

Sweet hour of prayer, sweet hour of prayer
That calls me from a world of care,
And bids me at my Father's throne
Make all my wants and wishes known:
In seasons of distress and grief
My soul has often found relief,

And oft escaped the tempter's snare
At thy return, sweet hour of prayer.
Sweet hour of prayer, sweet hour of prayer,
Thy wings shall my petition bear
To Him whose truth and faithfulness
Engage the waiting soul to bless:
And since He bids me seek His face,
Believe His Word, and trust His grace,
I'll cast on Him my every care,
And wait for thee, sweet hour of prayer.

From whom better to learn the New Testament method of the power of positive praying than the One seated at the right hand of the Father? Here are ten things to get us started.

1. **Jesus prayed in secret.** *"And when He had sent the multitudes away, He went up on the mountain by Himself to pray. Now when evening came, He was alone there"* (Matt. 14:23 NKJV).

The physical closet of prayer, as the closet of the heart, is imperative to a healthy prayer life. Prayer must become habitual. "To pray without ceasing" in *every* place is a constant attitude of the divine presence. But there is no substitute for the habitual practice of prayer in the *secret* place.

2. **He prayed before eating.** *"And Jesus took the loaves, and when He had given thanks He distributed them to the*

disciples, and the disciples to those sitting down and likewise of the fishes, as much as they would" (John 6:11 NKJV).

Discipline in "returning thanks" is basic training for the really big battles.

3. He prayed before the important events of His life. *"Jesus spoke these words, lifted up His eyes to heaven, and said: 'Father, the hour has come. Glorify Your Son, that Your Son also may glorify You, as You have given Him authority over all flesh, that He should give eternal life to as many as You have given Him'"* (John 17:1–2 NKJV).

Of greatest importance is that which glorifies the Father and reconciles men and women unto Him.

4. He prayed in times of great popularity. *"Then those men, when they had seen the sign that Jesus did, said, 'This is truly the Prophet who is to come into the world.' Therefore when Jesus perceived that they were about to come and take Him by force to make Him king, He departed again to the mountain by Himself alone"* (John 6:14–15 NKJV).

Do our successes drive us more to dependency on Him, or less?

5. He prayed in times of rejection. *"Then Jesus came with them to a place called Gethsemane, and said to the disciples, 'Sit here while I go and pray over there.' And He took with Him Peter and the two sons of Zebedee, and He began to be sorrowful and deeply distressed. Then He said to them, 'My* *soul is exceeding sorrowful, even to death. Stay here and watch with Me'"* (Matt. 26:36–38 NKJV).

Jesus needed His friends in His night of darkest sorrow as we need Him in ours.

6. **He prayed submissively.** *"He went a little farther and fell on His face, and prayed, saying, 'O My Father, if it is possible, let this cup pass from Me; nevertheless, not as I will, but as You will'"* (Matt. 26:39 NKJV).

"Not my will, but Thine" are our most important words in prayer.

7. **He prayed earnestly.** *"And being in agony, He prayed more earnestly. Then His sweat became like great drops of blood falling down to the ground"* (Luke 22:44 NKJV).

Shallow words move not the heart of God. The depth of soul behind our words stirs the heart of God.

8. **He prayed for His enemies.** *"Then Jesus said, 'Father, forgive them, for they do not know what they do.' And they divided His garments and cast lots"* (Luke 23:34 NKJV).

Loving those who don't love us may well be the ultimate validation of our faith.

9. **He never allowed a busy schedule to keep Him from prayer.** *"However, the report went around concerning Him all the more; and great multitudes came together to hear, and to be healed by Him of their infirmities. So He Himself often withdrew into the wilderness and prayed"* (Luke 5:15–16 NKJV).

Is our problem too little time to pray, or too little desire? If we will, we can always find time to pray.

10. **He prayed early in the morning.** *"And in the morning, rising up a great while before day, he went out, and departed into a solitary place, and there prayed"* (Mark 1:35 KJV).

> *"Those that seek me early shall find me."*
> *(Prov. 8:17 KJV)*

Following His example, you will find the sweetness of the early hours to be the best. When He is first in your day, you will be first in His. Jesus was our model and teacher in prayer. By His life and His lips our Lord's constant fellowship with the Father pointed to the necessity of ours. If He must pray, how much more must we, and that with all our hearts.

Jesus didn't pray merely as an example to us. For thirty-three years, He lived as a man, tempted in all points like as are we. He prayed because He had to pray. He prayed because He must. If the Son of God prioritized prayer, how much more must we? And His prayers were answered as will be ours, if like Him we pray in His will, in His Word, and in faith.

For that's the power of positive praying.

SECTION 1

FINDING

CHAPTER 1

FROM MY BIBLE

You can live in a state of constant abiding in Christ, with powerful answers to positive prayers you may have never experienced before, because you can know God's will unquestionably and pray positively.

The key to answered prayer is the divine formula:

God's will to bestow + *my* faith to believe = answered prayer.

Two major factors in knowing His will are hidden in an often quoted but easily overlooked treasure from Romans 12:1–2:

> *I beseech you therefore, brethren, by the mercies of God, that you **present your bodies a living sacrifice**, holy, acceptable to God, which is your reasonable service. And do not*

be conformed to this world, but be transformed
by the renewing of your mind, that you may
prove what is that good and acceptable and
perfect will of God. (NKJV, emphasis added)

The Beloved Apostle sets forth two important factors in knowing the will of God:

1. **The first is a disciplined, consecrated body.** The Bible has much to say about the body. The spiritual condition of the believer can be closely related to their physical condition.

Your body is the temple of the Holy Ghost.
(1 Cor. 6:19 KJV)

I keep under my body. (1 Cor. 9:27 KJV)

The relationship of body and soul may be far more important than we have ever imagined. God cares about the body He indwells. If you would sincerely know the will of God, first offer Him your body as a living sacrifice. Do everything you can to present it, the best possible specimen to God, keeping fit by exercise, sleep, healthy diet, and avoiding tobacco, alcohol, and drugs. The prize is worth the price.

Offering your body as a living sacrifice also includes the careful training of a keen and alert mind, a well-guarded tongue, and consecrated eyes and ears that speak, see, and hear only that which glorifies the Father.

2. **The other key is a separated life.** *"Adulteresses! Don't you know that friendship with the world is hostility toward God? So whoever wants to be the world's friend becomes God's enemy"* (James 4:4).

> *Do not love the world or the things that belong to the world. If anyone loves the world, love for the Father is not in him.* (1 John 2:15)

Worldly believers have clouded minds, divided hearts, and rebellious wills that can never clearly *know*, let alone *do*, the Father's will.

We also know God's will by "knowing Him." The apostle Paul longed to live a life of constant fellowship with the Lord. He wanted his desires, his ambitions, his will to cease to exist. He literally wished Paul might die and rise spiritually—a new Paul, totally yielded to the Father—*that he might experience what was potentially his in Christ. "But I make every effort to take hold of it because I also have been taken hold of by Christ Jesus"* (Phil. 3:12).

To enter into such resurrection oneness with Christ, he said, "I must be resurrected spiritually and so, first must die."

To die and live again like this, he said, is to *"know Him"*—*"That I may know him, and the power of his resurrection"* (Phil. 3:10 KJV).

In Genesis, we find the words, *"Adam knew Eve his wife; and she conceived, and bare Cain"* (Gen. 4:1 KJV).

In Luke, the angel told Mary she would give birth to a child. She used the same term. *"How shall this be, seeing I know not a man?"* (Luke 1:34 KJV).

To *know* obviously means "to be in union with." The relationship of the believer to Christ is as the relationship of husband and wife. They have the same name, the same bank account, the same possessions. What belongs to one, belongs to both. Legally, they are one. Emotionally, physically, mentally, spiritually in marriage, they are one. The union of two bodies becomes the physical instrumentality through which that union flows. Paul's prayer was to enter into the same deep union with Christ.

Have you ever known a couple, perhaps your grandparents or great-grandparents who have been married sixty or seventy years, who talk alike, act alike, think alike, and even look alike? Now that's scary! They have been one for so long, their desires and actions have been melted into perfect unity. Ask one what the other likes, thinks, feels, or believes, and they will know. Just so, to know God is to know His will.

And if you are not absolutely sure that you know Him, go talk to your pastor.

With Jesus, as with husband and wife, *time plus proximity equals sensitivity.* And security. I don't need to know where she is or what she's doing when she's out of my sight. After sixty years of wonderful marriage—not to worry—I know she's coming home. Like the disciples, we've walked together "side by side."

"Following Jesus" doesn't mean walking single file in a line behind Him. It means to honor Him, listen to Him, hear His teachings, and obey them.

And how could they hear twenty, thirty, forty feet in back of Him on a windy day by the sea?

I chuckle when I do so, but as they went along, I sometimes wonder if they, like Uldine and I, ever sang:

> *Oh we ain't got a barrel of money,*
> *Maybe we're ragged and funny.*
> *But we'll travel along, singin' a song,*
> *Side by side.*
> *Don't know what's comin' tomorrow,*
> *Maybe it's trouble and sorrow.*
> *But we'll travel the road, sharin' our load*
> *Side by side.*

Through all kinds of weather
What if the sky should fall.
Just as long as we're together,
It really doesn't matter at all.
When they've all had their quarrels and parted,
We'll be the same as we started.
Just travelin' along
Singin' a song,
Side by side.
—Harry M. Woods

Just so, through constant fellowship and daily communion with the Father, we can know how He thinks, what He desires, and what He wills because we *know Him.* Our union with Jesus has made us one.

And you can know the will of God by a deep, intuitive *sense of knowing* called *discernment.* It is a wonderful spiritual gift to the body of Christ, and some have it more than others. I call it "a holy hunch."

How do you know when you're hungry? You just know. How do you know when you're sleepy? You just know. The Quakers call it "minding the checks." In the depth of your spirit, God sometimes puts a holy hesitation. You're at peace or not at peace, and you just know to do it, or not to do it.

Isaiah 30:21 is God's special gift in our journey to find His will. *"And whenever you turn to the right or to the left, your ears will hear this command behind you: 'This is the way. Walk in it.'"*

Jesus said, "My sheep know My voice." It is a soft and gentle voice—not an audible, vocal voice but a deep, peaceful impression in the soul, *"This is the way. Walk in it."*

> *Take delight in the LORD, and He will give you your heart's desires. (Ps. 37:4)*

This, my favorite verse, is set in a context of several important words: *commit, trust, silent, wait.*

> *Take delight in the LORD, and He will give you your heart's desires. Commit your way to the LORD; trust in Him, and He will act. Be silent before the LORD and wait expectantly for Him; do not be agitated by one who prospers in his way, by the man who carries out evil plans. (Ps. 37:4–5, 7)*

The Hebrew word translated "give" means *to set—to hand to—to put.* So if you're absolutely crazy about Jesus and feel in your heart He really wants you to do something, go for it. He put it there. He's the One who put "the put" in your "go." Is that cool or what!

As two streams become one river, our spirits will become one. And *His will* becomes one with *our will*. His desires, our desire. I don't have to ask Uldine whether she wants to go night-clubbing or to the NASCAR races. After sixty years of marriage, I know her heart, and the answer is, "Neither."

Often a person will ask, "Is this or that God's will for me?" That's not the question. The question is, "Is Jesus Christ the delight and passion of my heart?" If the answer's yes, just do what you *want* to. You have sanctified your "wanter" by immersion into *His,* and what He wants will be what you want.

Another major factor in knowing the will of God is to be *willing* to do His will when you *do* know it. *"If any man will do his will, he shall know of the doctrine, whether it be of God, or whether I speak of myself"* (John 7:17 KJV, emphasis added).

For three years Jesus sought to convince the Jews He was the Son of God. Finally He turned to them and in essence said, "You don't *know* whether I am God's Son and whether My doctrine is God's because you don't *want* to know. You wouldn't honor Me if you did, so you are never going to know who I truly am. You must be *willing to know* or you *shall never know.*"

God will never impose the revelation of His will upon your predetermined will. Baker James Cauthen, at a conference of young pastors, once said, "Young men, you believe

God has called you to serve Him. What makes you think He put a sign at the border, 'Not Beyond Here'?"

You must be willing to know and do His will in advance. God won't pitch it until you put on your catcher's mitt.

I love the beautiful second verse of the old hymn, "Open My Eyes That I May See."

> *Silently now I wait for Thee*
> **Ready** *my God* **Thy will** *to see. (emphasis added)*
> —*Clara H. Scott*

A man clinging to the branch of a tree over the edge of a cliff asked God for help. God said, "I'll help you, but first let go of that branch." He thought about it and yelled out, "Anybody else out there?"

If you approach God expecting to have the right to trump His will, be ready for a very long and uncomfortable silence.

And remember that praying "if it be Thy will" and "Thy will be done" are quite different. If you already know God's will, why would you pray "if it be Thy will"?

If you don't know His will, the essential ingredient in learning it is having a surrendered will and a sensitive spirit. Then you can pray, "Thy will be done." You must submit your will to the Father's before He will reveal His to you.

Too often we pray, "Lord, this is what I want; let's hear what You have to say about it." You should never come to the Lord that way. Willingness to do His will before He reveals it is the basic requirement for His doing so.

A lady asked that I pray for her son to know God's will for his life because he was anxious to find out whether it was something he wanted to do or not. Both she and her son were wasting their time. We can't tell God what we want, to see if it fits into His plans; nor can we ask what He wants to see whether it fits into ours.

We can learn God's will through the counsel of godly people. *"The way of a fool is right in his own eyes, but he who heeds counsel is wise"* (Prov. 12:15 NKJV).

Ointment and perfume delight the heart, and the sweetness of a man's friend gives delight by hearty counsel. (Prov. 27:9 NKJV)

In 1972, I preached citywide crusades in Lagos, Port Harcourt, Ibadin, and Jos, Nigeria. Many thousands made decisions for Christ. For eleven months, I struggled over resigning my church and returning to Nigeria as a career missionary evangelist. I sought the counsel of legendary Nigerian missionary, Josephine Skaggs. "Bro. John," she said, "you can do more for missions by building a missionary church than by going yourself."

Forty-three years have proven her counsel to be invaluable. Over a thousand of our members have entered full-time ministry; one hundred twenty five to the international mission field and one hundred ten mission churches planted. Don't think I could have gone to all those countries or pastored all those churches.

I wrote my first *Power of Positive Praying* in Oklahoma City. I'm writing the new *Power of Positive Praying* in Houston. Let me tell you how I got from Oklahoma to Texas. Contemplating a move, the Lord impressed me to call a godly mature pastor friend for advice. Dr. W. T. Furr had the answer. "When God's in a move, two things will happen. No particular order, but they will both happen. A release from the old and a passion for the new."

Occasionally guidance may come unsought through another. In 1959, I was leading worship for evangelist Hyman Appleman in a crusade in Tulsa. I'd been seriously thinking about the call to preach. After the service, Pastor J. C. Sigler bounded onto the platform and out of the clear blue said, "Johnny, have you ever thought God might be calling you to preach?" and walked away.

But be careful here. God's voice is a soft impression, not a noisy gong.

When people say, "God impressed me," I listen.

When they say, "God told me," I walk away.

When they say, "God told me to tell you," I run.

CHAPTER 2

FROM MY EXPERIENCE

Essential in discerning God's will is watching His hand and reading circumstances. When you let God be God, He creates them as He opens and closes doors. You want to go where He leads. You want to work where He is at work.

We know we walk in His steps by carefully watching the way things providentially work out in keeping with His word.

> *Your word is a lamp to my feet and a light to my path. (Ps. 119:105 NKJV)*

"You don't have to force open any doors. God's doors open gently." And His lamp has a very strong bulb.

A person prayerfully seeking a job has three interviews for employment. One makes no response whatsoever. One promises to call back and never does. One offers the job. God's will? Take it. *Clarity comes through opportunity.*

In *Through the Looking Glass*, Alice meets the Cheshire Cat. She asked him which way she should go. He asked her where she wanted to go. She answered, "Oh, I don't much care where." To which the Cat responded, "Then it doesn't matter which way you go."

Not good advice.

No God in the equation—no clarity.

Paul and Timothy were forbidden by the Holy Spirit to go to Asia. But when they answered the Macedonian Call, they came "with a straight course" to Samothracia, Neapolis, and Philippi, the great city of Macedonia.

The expression "with a straight course," means "with the trade winds behind them." Through His open doors, the wind of the Holy Spirit blows real, real good.

And you can know the will of God by your own common sense, just figuring out some things for yourself.

Don't think that isn't being spiritual. Who do you think gave you the ability to reason? Who gave you the brains with which to do the figuring?

God will never reveal His will to you in some special way, if at birth He has already equipped you with what it takes to know His will.

You don't glorify God by standing on the street corner and praying for Him to tell you what time it is. He has given you eyes to see, money to buy a watch, and the ability to tell time. You don't have to pray about it. Just look at your watch.

If the light's red, don't pray about stopping. Stop. If it's green, go. If God has inherently equipped you with what it takes to know His will, it won't come to you through some divine revelation.

You can know the will of God through the Word of God.

> *All Scripture is inspired by God and is profitable for teaching, for rebuking, for correcting, for training in righteousness, so that the man of God may be complete, **equipped for EVERY good work**. (2 Tim. 3:16–17, emphasis added)*

And that includes God's guidance to His children.

God wants you to know His will *more than you want to know it* and is doing everything possible to make it clear. He isn't playing spiritual cat and mouse with you. Start the trip with a positive frame of mind and you're halfway home. We talk about "finding God's will." It's not really lost; it's *right in front of your eyes.*

God speaks to us through His Word. But two important factors should be remembered:

1. God's Word is not primarily a book of laws and rules, but where there are laws and rules they should be obeyed.
2. Basically, the Bible is a book of principles. The Bible does not say, "Thou shall not smoke." But the principle that tells me to *glorify God in my body* covers that. Nor does it say, "Thou shall do fifty push-ups a day," but I get it.

You don't need to pray about things God has already made clear. If the Word teaches us to seek Him early, and it does, you don't have to pray about it. Just get your head off the pillow and your knees on the floor. Early.

God's will is seen in God's Word through principles, concepts, and metaphors.

Jesus' statement, *"If thy right hand offends thee, cut it off,"* does not mean take an ax and chop away. It means, "Remove those things from your life which impede your spiritual growth into His likeness."

And learning the will of God is a progressive revelation. You can never see Point Z from Point A. Be faithful in what you do, with what you have, where you are.

Seek the Lord, read His Word, watch His hand, use the brains He gave you, and take *the next right step*. That step will be Point B. Only at Point B will you see Point C. And all the way to His perfect "Z."

Missionary evangelist Harvey Kneisel began his ministry in 1951, working his way through college. Each three summer months' employment at Shawnee Milling Company earned him the money for the following year's tuition. Freshman, sophomore, and junior.

At the beginning of his fourth summer, he was invited to preach a seven-day revival in Newkirk, Oklahoma. His boss said, "No way. If you leave, there'll be no job when you come back."

Harvey went to Newkirk and just last week said, "Bro. John, in sixty-three years I've never missed a single day of full-time ministry."

The Great Commission was "Mission Impossible."

It was physically impossible. The world hadn't even been discovered yet.

It was numerically impossible. They were too few.

It was financially impossible. They had no money.

It was legally impossible. It was against the law to "speak or teach in the name of Jesus."

It was socially impossible. Influence flows downhill. They were commoners. Who would listen to them?

Before they gave it up and went back to their fishing nets, I can just hear one of them say, "As one last gesture of honor to the Lord Jesus, let's do what He said. Let's go have that prayer meeting and take the next right step."

At Pentecost God brought the world to them.

And God reveals His will by His blessing or lack thereof.

If you're trying to decide between being a surgeon and a truck driver and everyone on whom you operate dies, better go "check out them eighteen-wheelers, Bubba."

CHAPTER 3

FIRST

Colossians 1:17 says, *"He is before all things and in Him all things consist."* He is before—preeminently *and* sequentially—everything in life. And allowing Him to be just that in your daily schedule is vitally important. Put Him first; He puts you first.

Nothing is more the heart of our relationship with Jesus than that beautiful word *first.* Decisions. Money. Purpose. Schedule. Everything. First. *"But seek **first** the kingdom of God and His righteousness, and **all these things** will be provided for you"* (Matt. 6:33, emphasis added).

Give Him the first day of the week, and He makes the other six far more blessed. The "Sabbath rest" principle changes everything. More blessed, more productive are six days under His Lordship than seven not.

The seventh year of rested land meant agricultural prosperity. Seven years without meant Babylonian captivity.

Give Him the firstfruits of your income, and He gives you not 90 percent, but 120 percent or 150 percent. *"Give, and it will be given to you; a good measure—pressed down, shaken together, and running over—will be poured into your lap. For with the measure you use, it will be measured back to you"* (Luke 6:38).

Give others forgiveness and God gives you forgiveness. *"For if you forgive people their wrongdoing, your heavenly Father will forgive you as well"* (Matt. 6:14).

Give Him the best of your service, and He gives you the best of positions. *"Whoever exalts himself will be humbled, and whoever humbles himself will be exalted"* (Matt. 23:12).

Here's the heart of it all.

Put God first; He puts you first.

Meet Him in the morning stillness,
    Before your hectic day.
He gently goes before you,
    And softly smooths the way.
Meet Him in the splendor of sunrise and sing,
    When morning guilds the skies,
    My heart awakening cries,
    "May Jesus Christ be praised!"

In the stillness of the morning, that's where you meet Him best.

And you don't have to prepare. You don't have to do anything. *Just show up.* Early. First thing. Just be with Him. Only Him. First.

He'll be waiting.

Wait before working and work so much easier. He sees you all day long, clothed in Himself, and it changes everything.

When your preeminent priority is Him, His preeminent priority is you.

He goes before you with hidden treasures all day long. And He has a wonderful plan for your life. Every hour of every day, day by day.

> *"For I know the plans I have for you"—this is the LORD's declaration—"plans for your welfare, not for disaster, to give you a future and a hope." (Jer. 29:11)*

> *I will instruct you and show you the way to go;* **with My eye on you,** *I will give counsel. (Ps. 32:8, emphasis added)*

Don't rush into your day. You face nothing alone. Don't try to hurry the process. He's trying to slow it down.

*At daybreak, LORD, You hear my voice; at
daybreak I plead my case to You and watch
expectantly. (Ps. 5:3)*

*After the earthquake there was a fire, but the
LORD was not in the fire. And after the fire
there was a voice, a soft whisper. (1 Kings
19:12)*

*Very early in the morning, while it was still
dark, He got up, went out, and made His way
to a deserted place. And He was praying there.
(Mark 1:35)*

He surrounds you twenty-four hours a day. He is in you,
with you, about you, before you.

In times of stress, draw back your mind to "the presence" of the morning and smile. Jesus is the Word—the
Logos—the living mind, heart, and soul of God. The Bible
is the written record of who Jesus is, what He did, what He
said, and what it means. To be absorbed in His Word daily,
early, first, is to be absorbed in Him.

On a beautiful Sunday morning in March 1965, I
preached my first sermon as a pastor. It was an exciting
time! All day long, my mind was exploding with ideas to
carry out, projects to start, things to do. I went to bed after

midnight with a list of seventeen things to do on Monday. I couldn't sleep. I was in the office before 6:30 a.m. and flew into action.

Goal? Finish the list, get everything done on that first Monday, get it over with, get it out of the way. Then I would have time the rest of my entire pastorate for family, people, prayer, Bible study—the really important stuff.

At a deeper level, I knew what was really important and I'd get to it real soon. But first I had to "do the list," do the pressing stuff, get it off my mind. I couldn't wait for Monday night so I could go to bed—mission accomplished—and start doing what really matters on Tuesday morning. This time the first things would indeed be first.

Fifty years, 18,250 nights, and 18,250 lists later, as I write these words, *the list* is still my biggest struggle. The immediate, the urgent, or the best, the eternal. I've never gone to bed without that list and often add to it throughout the night.

So how do I do in the battle for priorities? Guess I'd better fess up. It's about a 60/40 deal. He wins just a bit more often than the list.

But let me tell you what happens when "the Lord" wins out over "the list."

The list first. I'll get to the Lord later. I usually get through the list, but I'm a bit tired and frazzled and need a whole lot more time.

The Lord first. I'll get to the list second. The day is much shorter and I'm only a bit tired (but get much more accomplished). God's been before me and I can see it every step of the way.

What takes ten to twelve hours when "the list" wins, takes only about five to six when He wins.

And when the Lord wins out over the list, I see things every day that can only be explained by "that's a God thing." Here are just a few.

Over several months, I had unsuccessfully tried to make contact with six important people. Early one morning, I felt the Lord say, "Go see them." Five of the six were walking into the lobby of their office just as I came in. Nice visit. Mission accomplished. Almost. Five out of six ain't bad.

Two years of trying to make contact with Franklin Graham proved unfruitful. One morning in casual telephone conversation with a friend in Louisiana, I mentioned it. "Oh," he said, "Franklin is my best friend." Twenty minutes after we hung up, Franklin called me.

I inadvertently dropped a $17,000 cashier's check in the mailbox with several letters. The next morning the substation postmaster said, "By now it's downtown with millions of other pieces of mail." Eight hours later, the post office returned it to me—special delivery.

For our fiftieth wedding anniversary, I found the most perfect vintage necklace for Uldine you can imagine. Two months later, boarding a plane for Jackson, Mississippi, she lost it. Multiple trips to the airport "Lost and Found" were unproductive, as were endless searches of almost everything she owned. Six months later on Christmas Eve, she put on her favorite jacket, and there in that same pocket she had repeatedly searched was the necklace.

I called twenty-three car dealers and described the used car I was looking for—color, model, age, and mileage. I found only one: with thirty thousand miles. The next morning I drove to the dealership to see it, only six miles from my home. The salesman showed it to me. Then he said, "Now let me show you what *just came in* thirty minutes ago." It was the very car I wanted, three years old—with only twenty-six hundred miles on the odometer. That's right. Not twenty-six *thousand* but twenty-six *hundred*.

I like to hunt. Panic in society made .22 shells virtually impossible to buy. For weeks, I called everyone and looked everywhere—no shells. One afternoon driving to see our kids in Tyler, Texas, I felt impressed to pull over in Jacksonville, twenty-seven miles outside of Tyler. The thought came into my mind to call the local sporting goods store. They had none but told me about a small roadside resale shop, half a mile out of town they had heard had some shells. I was there in five minutes. The guy said, "Yeah, I've got forty-five boxes at home under my bed." I said, "I'll take 'em." The next morning he brought them. I bought them. (Actually there were fifty-two.)

I needed some paperwork from the courthouse for a new alarm system for our home. I'd been there before, and it's a menagerie of offices and long lines with one- to two-hour waits for virtually anything. Reluctantly I decided to make the trip. On a side street I saw a small building that said, "Courthouse Permits." It was a new building, and issuing permits was all they did. In five minutes I had the paperwork.

I called the only constable in our area to come to our home for the inspection. The alarm company told me it could be weeks before he even returned my call. I called him and left a message anyway. Five minutes later, he called me. One hour later, he was at our door.

I pulled into my bank to deposit a check at the drive-in window. A strong wind blew it out of my hand. It was circulating in the wind in front of the windshield, and I was parked too close to the teller's window to open the door and chase it. In less time than it takes to write it, the same wind that blew it away, blew it right back in my window.

I struggled to get the principle and interest to repay a loan from a friend. On the due date, I finally got it together and took it to him. He said, "Thanks, but no interest needed."

I bought some expensive hearing aids that are placed deep inside the ear and cannot be seen. I lost one soon after the one-year warranty expired. The audiologist said, "Not to worry, they come with a five-year insurance policy too."

We came home from a trip to find a sinkhole at the end of our driveway so large we couldn't even get into our garage. After days of trying to get to the right people to get it fixed, I picked up the phone to try one last time and looked out the window. They were fixing the sinkhole.

I searched for months for a particular type of box to hold my small collection of antique pens. One afternoon, we drove to Marble Falls, Texas, to see a dental specialist. Walking in to his office, I glanced in the window of a small store next door, and there was the box.

Uldine and I drove to Falls Creek Assembly in Oklahoma, sweating all the way because I had forgotten my registration papers to get through the security gate. When we arrived, the guards simply smiled and waved us through.

Three months ago I understood my ophthalmologist to say I had macular degeneration. A friend told me he had it too and said, "You'd better get serious and take care of it now. It'll never get better, but you can stop it from getting worse. To delay can be catastrophic."

Yesterday I left a message for Linda Rhodes, our ophthalmologist, and asked her to recommend a doctor for my surgery for macular degeneration because I was ready to get it done.

As I'm writing this chapter, she just called me back and said, "No, John, you've just got cataracts. We can fix that."

That was yesterday. You won't believe what happened today—as I'm still writing.

I sleep with a BIPAP machine. Somehow I lost the location of the store where I get my supplies. It was time for new supplies. For six weeks "it was time for new supplies." Three or four different times, I spent hours searching the part of our city where I *just knew* it was, trying to find the store. I know now why God blotted the memory of the place out of my mind. He wanted to show the great power of His hand. Sitting down to write this morning, out of nowhere (yes I know where) came a thought. It was extremely clear and accompanied by a warm glow. "I wonder if I forgot to mention my presidency of the Southern Baptist Pastor's Conference in the biographical sketch that

I send to my speaking engagements?" I walked over to my filing cabinet and pulled up the tab, BIO, for biography to check it out. Guess what's right next to "BIO"? "BIPAP." I excitedly opened the file and there was the name, address, and phone number of the BIPAP store, *complete with directions.* What can I say, but "Hallelujah!" I think that's Latin for "YAHOO!"

We went to visit Jerry and Joyce Witten for dinner. At the gate, I realized I didn't know their security code, nor did I have their phone number. As I sat at the gate, my cell phone rang. "Hey Bro. John, it's Jerry. Here's our security code."

Pray. Pray early. Pray first.

1. Abraham rose early to stand before the Lord. (Gen. 19:27)
2. Jacob rose early to worship the Lord. (Gen. 28:18)
3. Moses rose early to give God's message to Pharaoh. (Exod. 8:20)
4. Joshua rose early to capture Jericho. (Josh. 6:12)
5. Gideon rose early to examine the fleece. (Judg. 6:38)
6. Jesus rose early to pray. (Mark 1:35)
7. The women rose early and found the risen Christ. (Mark 16:2)

The power of positive praying is about finding God's will, walking in God's way, hearing God's Word, and doing it all *first*, every day of your life. First things, first; it's fantastic and it's fun. Find. First. Faith. Try it. And start today. Your phone will start ringing too.

CHAPTER 4

FAITH

You can't build faith in your heart unless you absorb the Word in your mind.

Answered prayer? It means, as we've already seen, first. And it means *in faith*. And how does faith come?

*Faith comes by **hearing** . . . the word of God.*
(Rom. 10:17 NKJV, emphasis added)

Ready for a surprise? The Bible says more about hearing the Word than reading it. That's right, *hearing it*. Not just Bible studies from it. Not just sermons from it. Hearing the Word. The Bible. Scripture. The Old Testament and the New.

I can't wait to tell you the most life-impacting truth I've discovered since our journey through the first *Power of Positive Praying.*

Hearing the Scripture has been for me exponentially more life impacting than *reading* it. Yes, I know "hearing the Word" means "obeying it," but I guess I'm an auditory learner, and I can't deny the overwhelming impact that hearing God's Word has had on my life over reading it.

Jesus is God in a body; the Bible is God in a book. To absorb the book at the deepest possible level is overwhelmingly impacting on your walk with The Master.

And it's not just the key to life; *it is life.* The living Word of God incarnate in Jesus. The written Word of God incarnate in you.

Positive praying. Positive living. It's not just the main thing; it's everything. Hearing it is for me the key and perhaps for you as well. Here's how it works.

I can't read anything, visually focus on anything without being conscious of everything going on around me. Impossible. Sorry, *no can do.* You're probably the same. So here's what you do.

- Buy the Bible on a set of four MP3 CDs. Christian bookstores have them for about $50 a set. Various voices and translations abound. I like Max McLean reading the King James Version.
- Wear a blindfold.
- Get a remote control.

- Settle back in your easy chair and get ready to fly to heaven.

Faith comes by hearing the Word of God. Prayer is a conversation. As you hear God's Word, pray it back to Him. And do it every day before everything else.

Let me be clear. I still write my sermons with an open Bible and various commentaries and word study books spread before me. But my morning devotional time, my "just for me" time, is *hearing* the Word of God. And it's been life changing.

Uldine sent our son Tony these Scripture verses to help him pray through some difficult times in college.

Father, I love You and praise You and thank You for Your Word and all of the promises we can claim from it as Your children. You have said when we trust You and rely on You, according to the Scripture, we cannot be shaken; for You, Lord, surround Your people (Ps. 125:1–2) and will keep my mind and soul in perfect peace (Isa. 26:3). I have the confidence that if I abide in You and Your Word abides in me, I can ask (John 15:7) anything in Your name (His name is His will); so, Father, I ask (fill in whatever the need is) so that You may be glorified in all that I do (John 14:13). Thank You, Jesus, for Your words of life; they are alive and active and full of power (Heb. 4:12), and they will never return void but will always accomplish (Isa. 55:11) that which they are sent to do. And I thank You that You are alert and active, watching over Your Word to perform it (Jer. 1:12). Your Word has been written that I may believe and receive life (John 20:31) and life more abundantly, to it's full (John 10:10). Today, Lord, I need Your power and blood and life in my mind, conscious and subconscious, heart, and soul. I ask You to bring all the facts I need to my remembrance. I thank You, Father, that whatever I do in word or deed, in Your name, You will work through me (Col. 3:17) and, Father, according to Your Holy Word, there is nothing too hard or too wonderful for You (Jer. 32:17). I believe Your will for my life at this time is these classes, these studies and tests, so, Lord, for Your Word and Your faithfulness, I thank You. I seek and enquire of You on the authority of Your Word that I shall not lack any beneficial thing (Ps. 34:10). For You are God—You spoke and it was done, You command and it stands fast (Ps. 33:9). I praise and thank You and pray that all this be done unto me according to Your Word and in Your name—Sweet Jesus. Amen.

And it changed Tony.

It's all about the power of the Word. The Word brings faith, and faith coupled with His will moves the hand of God. And for me hearing it transcends reading it.

Here's how the engrafted Word becomes the outgrafted Word in your life.

- You know God's will and pray in faith believing.
- Circumstances mean nothing.
- God's promises mean everything.

You don't enter a dark room, put your hand on the light switch, stand there, and say, "If the lights ever come on, I'll turn the switch." No. You turn the switch *first,* and *then* the lights come on. Commitment comes first. Confirmation comes second.

And remember, faith doesn't mean God "can." Faith means God "will."

Faith means you make no provision in case it doesn't happen. You act as though it were already done, for in God's mind, it is.

Abraham went out to a land, *he knew not where.* But God knew where.

The Lord said to Joshua, *"Go forward. All this land, I have given you."* God did not say, "All this land will I give you." *But "I have already given you."* Mission accomplished. It's yours; just go get it—*in faith*!

Moses came to the Red Sea, Pharaoh's army behind him, deserts and mountains around him, deep waters before him. He didn't say, "If that thing would ever split, I'd get in it." He said, "Stand still boys, and watch what God's gonna do." *"See the salvation of the LORD"* (Exod. 14:13 KJV).

At the tomb of Lazarus, Jesus did not ask the Father to hear Him; He thanked Him that He already had. *"So they removed the stone. Then Jesus raised His eyes and said, "Father, I thank You that You heard Me"* (John 11:41).

To the glory of God, our Lord did some amazing things at Houston's First Baptist. But during those thirty years, we never saw how we could do any of the things we did. We just did them. In faith.

In 1972, we came to our Red Sea. Packed out and running over, we couldn't ensure our own future because we didn't own one inch of parking in downtown Houston. We parked courtesy of First City National Bank parking garage next door to the church.

One day, a new Pharaoh could arise at First City who "knew not Johnny," and we'd be out of business. We had to move. We bought property at the most strategic corner in Houston.

The architect told us the buildings would cost $3.2 million. We worked, sweat, and "hoorayed" with the announcement that we had pledged the $3.2 million. Eight months later, plans were finished, and bids opened.

Houston was caught up in the worst inflation spiral in the history of the construction industry. Costs were going up nearly 10 percent a month.

The lowest bid was $8.1 million.

I told a hugely disappointed congregation the bad news and said, "It's your church and your money. I want *you* to make the decision whether we go forward—in faith."

Recounting the amazing history of the church, I preached about God's faithfulness through many crises across more than a century and a half.

As I finished, the choir began to sing the old gospel song "We've Come This Far by Faith." I sang the chorus as a solo. "Don't be discouraged by the trouble in the world. This ole' church will still be standin' when Satan's fiery darts have all been hurled."

Then the choir picked it up again, "Oh, oh, oh we can't turn back. We've come this far by faith."

The people stood to their feet and began to cheer.

Please don't tell my deacons because I don't think they remember, but we never voted to borrow the money, sign the contract, build the buildings and move. . . . We just did it. Eighteen thousand baptisms, five hundred million dollars, one hundred and ten mission plants, two schools, and more than a thousand in full-time ministry later, they are still going forward. Faith still looms large in the DNA of Houston's First.

Recently, Pastor Gregg Matte asked the church to pledge $15 million, above the budget, to plant multiple new campuses across Houston, North America, and around the world. They pledged $27 million. And gave it.

What a wonderful Lord we serve and how He loves to bless His children. His barns are full and running over with blessings just waiting to be poured out for those who claim them. Find His will and claim it in faith and live. Really live. You don't want to settle for God's second best.

Faith comes by hearing, and hearing by the Word of God. Spend the $50, get the CDs, and see if it's right for you.

Hearing the Word builds *faith*. Searching the Word finds *His will*. Put them together—*wow*!

SECTION 2

FORM

CHAPTER 5

THANK HIM

Gratitude to God is not only the privilege and responsibility but the most natural response of His children. Certainly God knows we are grateful for His blessings, but expressing it verbally not only blesses the great heart of God but ours as well.

The first step into God's presence is thanking Him.

I treasure a story my son-in-law Curt told me about our little great-grandson, Thaddeus Jonathan.

Riding home, arms loaded with presents from his fifth birthday party, he asked if he could stop at the store for just one more gift. "T.J.," Curt said, "You've got more toys than any little boy in Nebraska."

"Yes, Papa," he replied, "And I sure am *thankful*."

Somehow you know they're thankful, but isn't it cool to hear them say it?

A feller reluctantly went to counsel with his wife who complained, "I know he loves me, but he never says it."

He responded, "I told her I loved her twenty years ago when I married her. If anything changes, I'll let her know."

Not good enough.

I rather imagine the number of us who return to thank God is very small in comparison to the many who find it so easy to make our requests known to Him. Thanks should be offered not only for our personal blessings but for all those wonderful things we share with others. Thanksgiving for the sunshine, the beauties of creation, and all our mutual blessings is never out of order. Thanking God is a great antidote for depression, doubting, and complaining.

> *Rejoice in the Lord always. Again I will say, rejoice! Let your gentleness be known to all men. The Lord is at hand. Be anxious for nothing, but in everything by prayer and supplication, with thanksgiving, let your requests be made known to God; and the peace of God, which surpasses all understanding, will guard your hearts and minds through Christ Jesus. (Phil. 4:4–7 NKJV)*

As you begin to thank God, pause and let Him remind you of every blessing. Two categories are helpful here—physical blessings and spiritual blessings.

We have many "take for granted" blessings for which to say, "Thanks."

Perhaps nothing is as old yet relevant as "I complained because I had no shoes until I met a man who had no feet." When you pray, name every physical blessing you enjoy. Thank God for your health and your family's. Thank Him for the perfection of their bodies. You say, "My child was born autistic," but millions were not born at all.

Thank Him for the little things. Don't think a $1,000 bill would do you much good at a hamburger stand. You're gonna need some change.

Thank Him for your clothes, your home, your car, your possessions, your jewelry, your furniture, the food in your pantry, and your money in the bank.

Perhaps you are thinking, *But I only have fifty dollars.* Some people only have five dollars. Perhaps you have only five dollars. There are people who would take a life for that amount of money.

Jesus taught us to celebrate small things. Sparrows, grass, bread, life, flowers, salt.

Little things become big things. Seeds become trees. Grains of wheat will one day feed five thousand. Cups of water gain disciples rewards.

> Little drops of water, little grains of sand,
>   Fill the might ocean, makes the mighty land.
> Little acts of kindness, little things you do.
>   Add up to the big things and makes all things
> new. —Julia Carney

Gratitude overcomes depression. Still grumbling over that old clunker? Ask ten young men on the streets of America, and you will find all ten can drive a car. Ask ten young men the same question in many other countries, and only one in ten will know how to drive. Why learn to drive a car when you'll never be able to afford one.

Little things are important. Every drop of blood contains millions of cells.

And thank God for your spiritual blessings. Thank Him for Himself, for His Son—for His life, death, and resurrection. Thank Him for your own personal experiences with Him, your own salvation. Thank Him for the Spirit of God who led you to Him and the person He used.

Express your heartfelt thanks to God. Think about it all day long as you think about Him.

Thank God for your church—the building and every person in it. Thank Him for the staff, teachers, deacons, and elders who serve long and faithfully. Thank God for your pastor, his wife, and family.

Memorize and pray the opening verses of one of the best loved psalms, *"Bless the Lord, O my soul; and all that is within me, bless his holy name! Bless the Lord, O my soul, and forget not all His benefits: who forgives all your iniquities, who heals all your diseases, who redeems your life from destruction, who crowns you with lovingkindness and tender mercies"* (Ps. 103:1–4 NKJV).

Express your heartfelt thanks to God. Thank Him for His joy. His peace. His leadership. Think about it all day long, and as you think about Him, sing it.

- Out loud.
- On our knees.
- In your heart.
- In your car.
- Everywhere.
- All the time.

I love to drive, and I love to sing as I do. And you know what? I think God loves it too.

Years ago, several Northwestern University students jumped into the freezing waters of Lake Michigan to rescue passengers from a capsized tour boat. Student Edward Spencer saved the lives of seventeen persons. Years later, R. A. Torrey told that story in a sermon.

"Bro. Torrey," someone shouted from the congregation, "Edward Spencer is here tonight." Dr. Torrey called the student to the platform amid the thunderous applause of the people. Later, he would tell the preacher, "Thank you so much. None of the seventeen ever thanked me."

CHAPTER 6

PRAISE HIM

Who wouldn't thank you for inviting them to dinner? But wouldn't it be more meaningful if they would brag on you, compliment you for your great cooking, and praise you for your beautiful home and hospitality?

Praising God is going the second mile. The first step into His presence is thanking Him. The second, praising, goes much farther. Giving God gratitude opens the door. Giving Him praise walks through it.

King David said it beautifully in Psalm 100:4, *"Enter His gates with thanksgiving and His courts with praise. Give thanks to Him and praise His name."*

Ancient cities were surrounded by a mighty wall and outer gates. Through them came merchants, strangers, and travelers. Virtually anyone could enter the public outer court through its mighty gates.

But to come into the intimate presence of the king, one must enter the smaller courtyard surrounding his palace. One entered the city through its outer gates. They proceeded into the presence of the king through his inner court.

Lots of people thank God publicly. We even have a national holiday for Thanksgiving. Sadly, its priorities, in order, are food, football, family, and faith.

Few people praise God personally, and praise is where He lives. God inhabits the praise of His people (Ps. 22:3).

It can be a bit difficult to pray with all your heart in front of others and almost impossible to pray an unaffected prayer in a church service. One cannot help but be conscious of their surroundings, especially the ears of other people. We may find ourselves praying more *for* people than *to* God when we pray in public.

1. **Look for physical solitude.** Get away from people and things. Go into another room, shut the curtains, and close the door to find quietness. If you are tempted to look around, bury your head in a pillow or use a blindfold. Put cotton in your ears. Shutting *out* the sounds and sights God has created makes it easier to be shut *in* with the Creator.

2. Have the same place to pray each morning. Choose a chair, a corner of the bed, a certain spot in your room or prayer closet and find a comfortable position. Pillows under your knees can make prayer more inviting. (There is no piousness in being uncomfortable when you pray.) Go to the same place at the same time in the same position every day, and prayer will become a habit, delightfully inviting and hard to break. Consistency is important.

3. Before you begin to talk to God, whether audibly or in your heart, relax a moment. Don't rush into the presence of God. Take a few deep breaths. Let your mind be quiet and your body relaxed. Wait a moment that you may know the conscious presence of Him who said, *"Be still, and know that I am God"* (Ps. 46:10 NKJV).

Have you ever been somewhere and not really been there at the same time? A man was apprehensive about taking his first plane ride. When he landed, someone asked him if he enjoyed it. "It wasn't as bad as I expected," he said, "but then I never did put all my weight down on that seat." We've all been before God but not totally committed to the moment.

By valuing the time I spend alone with the Lord, I enter His presence focused completely upon Him. By being still and blocking out distractions, I am declaring His value in my life.

We become accustomed to having everything at our fingertips—really fast. In less time than it takes to tell it, you can go around the world and find out everything about anything. Don't take your *Internet* mind-set into the *inner* presence of Jesus.

In three years of earthly ministry, Jesus moved in peace. He was never hurried, worried, rushed, or anxious. Two thousand years later, He still isn't.

In his beautiful hymn "This Is My Father's World," Maltbie Davenport Babcock wrote, "In the rustling grass I hear Him pass, He speaks to me everywhere."

Don't rush. Slow down and listen. Just listen.

I can imagine the children of Israel at the Red Sea organizing their armies, maneuvering their chariots. Suddenly Moses says, *"Stand still, and see the salvation of the LORD"* (Exod. 14:13 KJV).

Being still precedes seeing the power.

In the old days if someone missed the stagecoach, they simply waited five days for another. Today, if we have to wait five seconds in a revolving door, we have a panic attack. The spirit of the Lord moves upon peaceful waters. Slow down. Get quiet before Him. Get alone with Him and sense the reality of His presence. Now you are ready to pray.

The first two steps in prayer are thanksgiving and praise. The third is dealing with our sins.

I would suggest you not begin your prayer with the confession of sin. Why do most of us start that way? Probably because David said, *"If I regard iniquity in my heart, the Lord will not hear me"* (Ps. 66:18 KJV). But what did he mean? If I simply *have* any sin in my heart, God will not hear my prayer; therefore I must confess it first or God will not hear the rest of my prayer? No, he doesn't mean if I merely *have* iniquity in my heart.

The word *regard* means "retain." If I *retain* sin in my heart, God will not hear me. If I covet some sin, if I harbor it in one corner of my heart and refuse to let it go, *then* He will not hear me. If we only pray when no sin is in our heart, I fear we shall never pray at all.

If you begin your prayer by confessing your sins, you will find yourself in an unpleasant frame of mind, your prayer less inviting, and you won't pray very long. Begin on high. Start positively. Begin with thanksgiving and praise, and you won't want to stop.

When God changed my life through faith in Christ, He put a spring in my step, a song in my heart, a smile on my face, and a great desire to praise Him.

Praising makes you happy. It takes sixty-one facial muscles to frown and only twelve to smile. Praising God brings Him into the equation.

Pastor Chuck Smith used to say, "We never use a printed order of service. We just sing 'til God shows up. When everybody starts smiling, I start preaching."

Are you like Martha, so busy serving you have no time to sit at His feet and praise Him? Well that's too busy.

A friend and his wife flew to Beijing on a business trip. Every time something good happened, they would say, "Oh, praise the Lord."

"You Christian?" said the lady seated next to them.

"Yes, we are," they smiled.

"Oh, will you teach my little girl to sing praise songs to Jesus in English?"

And they did. All the way to China—and to the hotel. It was the highlight of their trip.

But do you just say, "Praise the Lord, Praise the Lord," over and over again? No. There are three wonderful ways to praise the Lord—

In your own words,

With psalms

With music

Mary said, *"My soul doth magnify the Lord"* (Luke 1:46 KJV). The psalmist said, *"My soul shall make her boast in* the LORD: *the humble shall hear thereof, and be glad"* (Ps. 34:2 KJV). How would you define *boast?* Is there any better definition than bragging? That's what praising the Lord is—bragging on Jesus.

And it's not because *He needs it;* it's because *we need it.*

What do you think of when you think of magnifying the Lord? To magnify is to enlarge something out of true perspective. Were you to brag on me or I on you, we could easily overdo it. Not so with Jesus.

There are two types of praise in which God delights, an *offering* of praise and a *sacrifice* of praise. Offerings of praise are when we shout our thanks in moments of appreciation and celebration of who He is and what He's done.

A sacrifice of praise comes at a price. We may be either ashamed to give, afraid to give, or too hurt to give it because of unpleasant circumstances, but we do so anyway.

In biblical days, a family was required to bring an animal sacrifice, always the best, often a pet. When we give a sacrifice of praise, we're not praising from the joy of life but from the heartbreak.

Praising God in the midst of sorrow, pain, loss, and defeat is difficult praise. It says to God: "I can't see You but I know You're there. Though I don't feel Your presence, I know You're with me. Though I can't hear You, I know You hear me."

Praise from the overflow is praise of joy. Praise from the emptiness is praise of faith. Offer Him your praise in both. He wants to hear it, and we need to give it.

Our God inhabits praise. The way to find someone at home is to go to where they live. Praise Him. Tell the Lord how great He is. Tell Him in your own words. You don't have any trouble bragging on a friend. Think of the greatness and goodness of our majestic Lord, and praise Him for every facet of His being and mighty works the Spirit of God brings to your mind.

Praise God through the Psalms. Turn almost anywhere in the Psalms and find a song of praise. As you kneel before Him, open your Bible and turn at random through the hymnal of the Bible. Pick out a good verse. Read it aloud. Read it again. Memorize it. Look up and say it to God. Make it your own. Say it in your own words. Repeat it. It will suggest others.

I love to see people lift their hands in praise, but it should never be simply a *primer* to get the praise flowing. It should be the *effect* of praise, not the *cause*. And of course, lifting up holy hands really means *lifting up a holy life*.

Praise God through music, not in the choir, not in the praise band, or in the church, but right there on your knees. If you can sing, sing. If not, say the words. If you want to sing out loud, sing!

Many wonderful songs will rise from our heart as we praise the Lord.

> *We praise Thee, O God!*
> *For the Son of Thy love,*
> *For Jesus who died,*
> *and is now gone above.*
>
> *We praise Thee, O God!*
> *For Thy spirit of light,*
> *Who has shown us our Savior,*
> *and scattered our night.*
>
> *Hallelujah! Thine the glory,*
> *Hallelujah! Amen.*
> *Hallelujah! Thine the glory,*
> *Revive us again.*
> *—William P. Mackay*

And pray the Word.

> *I will bless the LORD at all times: his praise shall continually be in my mouth. (Ps. 34:1 KJV)*
>
> *Make a joyful shout to God, all the earth! Sing out the honor of His name; make His praise glorious." (Ps. 66:1–2 NKJV)*

Bless the LORD, O my soul: and all that is within me, bless his holy name. Bless the LORD, O my soul, and forget not all his benefits. (Ps. 103:1–2 KJV)

Behold, bless the LORD, all you servants of the LORD, who by night stand in the house of the LORD! Lift up your hands in the sanctuary, and bless the LORD. The LORD who made heaven and earth bless you from Zion. (Ps. 134:1–3 NKJV)

I will praise You with my whole heart; before the gods I will sing praise to You. (Ps. 138:1 NKJV)

I will extol You, my God, O King; and I will bless Your name forever and ever. Every day I will bless You, and I will praise Your name forever and ever. Great is the LORD, and greatly to be praised; and His greatness is unsearchable. (Ps. 145:1–3 NKJV)

Praise the LORD! Praise God in His sanctuary; praise Him in His mighty firmament! Praise Him for His mighty acts; praise Him according to His excellent greatness! Praise Him with the sound of the trumpet; praise Him with the lute and harp! Praise Him with the timbrel and dance; praise Him with stringed instruments and flutes! Praise Him with loud cymbals; praise Him with clashing cymbals. Let every thing that has breath praise the LORD. *Praise the* LORD. *(Ps. 150 NKJV)*

A new convert kept saying, "Hallelujah! Hallelujah!" Someone asked if he knew what *Hallelujah* means. "I'm not sure," he said, "but I think it means 'hot dog, I've got it!'"

Now that's a "maybe so" and a "maybe no." But start somewhere, my brother and my sister, and praise the Lord. And remember, you can't praise Him too much.

CHAPTER 7

TELL HIM

First John 1:9 is just about the best news you'll ever hear. *"If we confess our sins, He is faithful and just to forgive us our sins, and to cleanse us from all unrighteousness"* (NKJV).

A careful study of each word will reveal some important truths. The first one's kind of *iffy.*

The forgiveness of our sins is conditional upon our repentance and confession. "If we confess." The very next verse makes our sins even "badder."

> *If we [believers] say we have not sinned, we*
> *make him a liar, and his word is not in us."*
> *(1 John 1:10 KJV)*

The unbeliever must deal with his *sin*, that he is a sinner by nature. The believer must deal with his *sins*, that he continues the practice of sin.

Forgiveness of the *guilt of our sin* is automatic upon conversion; unfortunately, death to the *practice of our sin* is not. The guilt of the old sin nature has been crucified. The practice of it must be being crucified every hour of every day.

> For I know that in me (that is, in my flesh) nothing good dwells; for to will is present with me, but how to perform what is good I do not find. For the good that I will to do, I do not do; but the evil I will not to do, that I practice. Now if I do what I will not to do, it is no longer I who do it, but sin that dwells in me. O wretched man that I am! Who will deliver me from this body of death? I thank God—through Jesus Christ our Lord! (Rom. 7:18–20, 24–25 NKJV)

I have been saved from the *penalty* of sin; I am being saved daily from the *power* of sin. Spiritual growth is a life-long process. Less sin, less often, means I'm making progress. It's called sanctification.

As children of God, we live in a state of relationship with God, which *cannot* be broken. We also live in a state of fellowship, which may *easily* be broken.

When I was a teenager, my dad managed a poultry farm in Kansas. My responsibility was to clean out from under the chicken coops. As you can imagine, it was quite disgusting. When I came home, my mom made me strip down in the backyard, leave my clothes, shoes, and residue outside. Only then could I come in and take my bath. The mess from the day had no place inside the house for the evening. Only after the bath was I permitted to join the rest of the family.

She didn't love me less, nor was I discarded from the family; it just wasn't acceptable to come into their presence in that condition. There was a distinct separation in our fellowship but not our relationship.

So it is with God. To restore fellowship with Him, He must forgive our sins, strip us down, and give us a good spiritual bath.

When my children disobey me, I correct them and certainly don't give them everything they want. This doesn't mean they are no longer my children; rather we are out of fellowship.

The next word in our verse is *we. "If we confess our sins,"* and it includes *all* believers.

We might be shocked to know how many *sins* are piled up between ourselves and our God because we have never learned to confess them individually. You may not have been in perfect fellowship with Him, had every sin forgiven, for many months or even years.

Daily asking God to forgive our *sins* in general is not enough.

Sometimes we pray, "Lord, forgive me of the sins I have committed and those I didn't know were sins." But you don't have to pray that way. If you wait patiently before the Lord, He will bring them to your memory and place the gentle finger of His convicting Spirit on each and every one.

In 1959, I went to the great Bellevue Church in Memphis to preach a Saturday youth retreat and Sunday night service. When he picked me up at the airport Friday afternoon, I asked the youth pastor if he had the key to the church that we might go pray at the pulpit. He did, and for two hours we did.

Later he would say, "I've never heard a man so openly confess his sins, including having glanced at a men's magazine on the way over." At the retreat and evening service about four hundred persons were saved, including twenty-two sailors from the Memphis Naval Base and about sixty other adult men and women. I'd say being open and honest with God about our sins is rather important.

Living with unconfessed, unforsaken sin is like living over a landfill. It matters not how stylish the landscape, manicured the grass, or lush the foliage above, the nuclear waste and limitless toxins beneath are still fatal.

Too many lives are like landfills. Beneath the surface lies the junk of disappointment and discouragement, lust and lying, pride and prejudice.

Remember the story of Joshua at Ai? One small sin can have large ramifications.

Legendary missionary Bertha Smith spoke in chapel at a great seminary. The first words from Miss Bertha were, "Boys, are your sins confessed up-to-date?" Miss Bertha got it right.

And our sins must not simply be considered, but confessed.

To biblically *confess* doesn't mean merely to acknowledge. It also means to change. Admitting all my sins on Facebook won't do the job.

To confess means "to agree with God as to His opinion of."

In the Roman Empire, people would often disagree as to the real winner of a chariot race. Their angle of sight might not let them clearly see the result. So a judge was placed at the perfect angle at the finish line to give the final word. This is the idea of which John writes. To agree with God means to see our sins from God's angle, to see them as the Judge of the Universe sees them.

Pray that God will give you a holy hatred for sin. If you would see sin as God sees it, go not to skid row, the brothel, or the alley but to Calvary, and there see the cross from God's perspective. Calvary is the epitome of God's love for the sinner and hatred for his sin.

If a drunk driver kills your child, you will forever have a different view of alcohol.

Some Christians evaluate their sins by society's standards. Public opinion changes with fads and whoever is "hot" at the moment or whatever is politically correct.

Putting a label "Dr. Pepper" on the outside doesn't change the deadly nature of a bottle of strychnine.

Some Christians evaluate their sins by their friends. Whatever is acceptable to "the gang" is appropriate behavior.

Some Christians evaluate their sins by other Christians. That's precisely what the Pharisees did. They flaunted their lives as better than others simply because they had ritualistic practices common people could not do.

If we bypass God's opinion of our sin and ask the opinion of everyone else about the seriousness of it, we'll lose the perspective that matters. God is the Judge and has never delegated that position to another.

Why do we sin? Because we are forced to? No. We sin because it pleases us; we sin because it satisfies us. We lie because it protects us. We are proud because we love ourselves. We indulge ourselves because we pamper our flesh. That is the way we look at our sins, not the way God does. Confession is more than simply telling God what He already knows.

When we do this, we have the assurance of His Word that He accepts our confession, and our sins are forgiven. Don't doubt God. Take Him at His Word.

Remember when you held your firstborn in your arms and said, "It doesn't feel like he's really mine?" But he was yours—not because you felt like it or didn't feel like it but because the law of physical birth had taken place.

So it is with the forgiveness of our sins. When they are confessed and genuinely forsaken, His forgiveness is not contingent upon our feelings but upon the fact of His Word. *"If we confess our sins, He is faithful and just to forgive us our sins and cleanse us from all unrighteousness"* (1 John 1:9 NKJV).

God said it, I believe it, and that settles it. In fact, that settles it whether I believe it or not.

There are two kinds of conviction for sin. Conviction is that troubled feeling that we have done wrong and need its guilt removed.

Conviction means "to make *aware* of, to be *reminded* of our sins, *before* we confess them." That conviction is from the Holy Spirit of God and is no small matter. When you are reminded of the slightest wrong, forsake it, confess it, repent of it, kill it, despise it, destroy it, else the sore may become a cancer, the thought a personality, the deed a life.

If conviction remains *after* we have confessed our sins, one of two things is true. Either it was not true confession, or the conviction is coming from somewhere other than the Holy Spirit.

In the latter case, it is from Satan. He is our accuser and takes no small delight in constantly troubling us over the memory of past sins. If you find this to be a problem, remember the words of James, *"Resist the devil, and he will flee from you"* (James 4:7 KJV).

Just say, "Devil, you cannot deceive me. Satan, you are a liar. You cannot convict me; my sins are confessed and forgiven. Jesus died for them, I have repented of them, and they are under the blood." You will find him to be a coward.

Quote 1 John 1:9 out loud, *"If we confess our sins, He is faithful and just to forgive us our sins and to cleanse us from all unrighteousness"* (NKJV). Satan is a liar. God's Word is the truth. The devil cannot resist the Word of God.

If conviction of past sins you know to be forgiven persists, write down the sin or sins that trouble you on a piece of paper, go to the sink, turn on the faucet, light a match, and burn the paper. As the flame engulfs the paper, pray out loud, "Lord, just as surely as the fire burns this piece of paper, I claim the all-powerful cleansing blood of Christ Your Son to destroy my sins forever." What your eyes see will help your heart know what your mind already believes.

There are three kinds of sins that require three types of confession:

1. There is *personal* sin, which no one knows about but you, and should only be confessed to the Lord.
2. There is *private* sin, which you and someone else know about. It is not enough to confess it to God, it should be confessed and made right with the other person.
3. There are *public* sins. If everyone knows about your sin, they have been spiritually offended, and your testimony impaired. It is not enough to confess it to God; it should be confessed publicly and restitution made.

A good principle to follow in the confession of sins is this:

1. Don't make the confession of the sin worse than it is, but do make it as bad as it is.

2. Make certain restitution has been made to those who have been offended.
3. Public confession of personal sin is never wise and usually does more harm than good.

When we receive Jesus, His cleansing blood *actually makes* the blackness of our sins as white in His eyes as the new fallen snow. Claim it, rejoice in it, live in it.

> *If we say that we have no sin, we deceive ourselves, and the truth is not is us. (1 John 1:8 KJV)*

But *"the blood of Jesus Christ His Son cleanses us from all sin"* (1 John 1:7 NKJV).

CHAPTER 8

Ask Him

Our Lord loves to hear "the ask."

"Give us this day our daily bread" means everything we need for physical life. David said, *"I have been young, and now am old; yet have I not seen the righteous forsaken, nor his seed begging bread"* (Ps. 37:25 KJV). God takes care of His kids.

Though you never again ask for water or thank Him for it, you will probably never die of thirst. But while asking for everyday needs may not necessarily be the means by which we *receive* them, it is certainly the means by which we *remember* where they come from. The atheist down the street will probably live physically as well as you, perhaps even better; but if you ask God for your daily bread, you will be more blessed than he. If my children never ask for a thing, I'll give them everything they need and more, but how much better will it be if they develop genuine appreciation for the gift and its source.

Two kinds of asking will be helpful: *petition* and *intercession*.

Petition is praying for ourselves. Our personal requests may be classified as both physical and spiritual. Paul said, *"My God shall supply all your need according to his riches in glory by Christ Jesus"* (Phil. 4:19 KJV).

You wouldn't hire a housekeeper and not give them the cleaning supplies to do their job. You may be certain that if something is necessary to carry out His will in your life, God is ready to give it. *"Now this is the confidence that we have in Him, that if we ask any thing according to His will, He hears us"* (1 John 5:14 NKJV).

Whatever God has called you to do, He will, with the call, give you the provision to accomplish.

Intercession is praying for others. You can be assured you pray in faith and in the will of God when you pray, *"Thy kingdom come. Thy will be done in earth"* (Matt. 6:10 KJV).

His will is for justice, charity, peace on earth, and goodwill to men, for He is indeed a good God. But He often awaits our prayers to exact it. You can pray in faith when you pray for men to be reconciled to each other, broken homes to be mended, and lives racked by disappointment and failure to find peace with God. You can pray for spiritual power and blessings upon loved ones, friends, and your church, in complete faith when you pray, *"Thy will be done in earth."*

Intercession, praying for others, may be the greatest ministry in the Kingdom. Only eternity will reveal what has been wrought by the prayers of God's people all over the earth whose names have never been heralded before the public.

The Bible admonishes us to intercede for:

- All in authority. (1 Tim. 2:2)
- Ministers. (Phil. 1:19)
- God's people. (Ps. 122:6)
- Servants. (Luke 7:2–3)
- Masters. (Gen. 24:12–14)
- Children. (Matt. 15:22)
- Our fellow countrymen. (Rom. 10:1)
- The sick. (James 5:14)

To name a few.

As you intercede for others, name those for whom you are praying and ask God to deal with their heart. Then rather than repeat the petition over and over, turn the spotlight of prayer on your own heart and spend most of your time letting God empty you, cleanse you, and fill you that you might be the instrument *through which* that one is touched.

Three entities are involved in praying for others: God, you, and the individual. If the person remains untouched after you have prayed, does the problem lie with God? Does He not care, or is He powerless to deal with that person? No. God is all powerful and all compassionate.

Is the problem with the unsaved one? Is his heart too hard? No. The sunshine of God's love is able to melt the hardest heart.

The problem may well lie with us. When the Holy Spirit first came into my heart and did the work of regeneration, He took up permanent residence. However, rather than filling and overflowing me that I may be His instrument of blessing to others, He is often crowded into one corner of my heart, and I become a dam of blockage rather than a channel of blessing.

"Do not grieve the Holy Spirit" (Eph. 4:30 NASB), and *"Do not quench the Spirit"* (1 Thess. 5:19 NASB). Sin, worldliness, faithlessness—all these things grieve and quench Him such that He is unable to flow freely through us.

How does the Spirit of God move in a church service? How does He deal with the unbeliever? Is it through the PA system, the pulpit, or the lights? God seldom uses things. *He uses us.* He must have someone who will offer himself a conduit for the Holy Spirit. Jesus said, that from within him *"shall flow rivers of living water"* (John 7:38 KJV).

What a promise! What potential! But in reality there is barely a trickle of power flowing through most of us and little outward fruit of the indwelling Spirit of God. We probably need not pray for others as much as for ourselves. The world has yet to see what God can do with one person completely yielded to Him.

A stone struck mighty Goliath in his temple. Was it the slingshot or the boy that held it that slew the giant?

At the great wedding in Cana of Galilee, six stone water pots became filled with about 150 gallons of wine. Was it the vessels that held the water, or Mary who asked, and the servants who filled them, that produced the results?

A tiny mask covers the mouth and nose of the surgeon to purify the air in the operating room. Is it the mask or the doctor's choice to wear it that protects the patient?

We are His instruments. And unconfessed sin in our lives is like corrosion on a battery cable that keeps the electrical current from getting from the generator to the battery.

George Harris was pastoring a large church in Mount Pleasant, Texas. He and Linda flew to Arizona to consider a very small church.

A thousand people or a hundred?

Sitting on the runway preparing to fly back to Texas, George said, "Honey, I love the city. I love the beautiful air, the mountains, the buildings, the people, *but the congregation is so small.*"

"George," she said, "the only thing you *want* to change is the only thing you *can* change. You."

They moved to Arizona.

And whatever you do, don't let go. In Matthew 7:7, Jesus said, *"**Ask** and you shall receive. **Seek** and you shall find. **Knock** and the door shall be opened to you"* (emphasis added).

Ask, seek, and *knock.* Each of these words is in the aorist future perfect verb tense in the Greek, which means keep on asking—keep on seeking—keep on knocking.

After you make your petition to God, you are still not finished with all *asking* means. One final step remains—the affirmation that your prayer will be answered. Have you really prayed in faith? Are you confident your requests lie within the will of God? Then you need not hesitate to thank Him that He is going to answer.

When you go to the bank to cash a check, you don't hesitate to expect the funds. Why? Because you have confidence in the one who wrote the check and the bank's ability to fund it. You simply present your claim and expect the results. To thank God in advance is to affirm your confidence in the forthcoming answer.

If you pray for someone who is sick, don't labor over thoughts and prayers of their sickness. Pray and think of the health Christ gives. When you think of one with a broken arm, don't think of the break, but pray and thank God for His healing power and the glory God will receive in their healing. That is positive praying.

Every year mine disasters occur around the world. Over and over comes the good news that a hole is being bored through the earth and air and supplies are being sent down to the miners. The work of the intercessor is drilling a hole of positive faith through the barriers of doubt and sin that shroud the one for whom we pray, that the supply of God's love may bear in upon them.

When you finish your prayer of intercession, don't get up—stay on your knees and thank God in advance that He has already answered your prayer. Get up, go your way, and don't check up on God or make other provision in case it doesn't happen.

Believe Him, thank Him, and leave it there.

CHAPTER 9

HONOR HIM

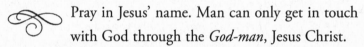 Pray in Jesus' name. Man can only get in touch with God through the *God-man*, Jesus Christ.

Too often at sporting events and civic gatherings, someone will finish their prayer, "And dear Lord, bless us today. Amen." Nothing leaves me flatter. I want to hear someone pray—God implores that we pray—in Jesus' name.

You may say, "But everything I do is in His name, and I feel in my heart I pray in His name." Yes, but while it is indeed *more* than those three words "in Jesus' name" at the end of a prayer, rather what they *mean*, we should still verbally *pray in the name of the Lord Jesus*.

To pray in Jesus' name means simply to pray on the merits of and through Jesus. It is to desire what He desires, to pray what He wants because of who He is and what He has done.

The Bible promises much in the name of Jesus. *"There is none other name under heaven given among men, whereby we must be saved"* (Acts 4:12 KJV). And again, *"Whosoever shall call upon the name of the Lord shall be saved"* (Rom. 10:13 KJV).

Why is so much promised through the name of Jesus Christ? A name is the person it represents. If someone says the name "Barbara," it means nothing to me. If they say the name "Hazel," still there is nothing. But when someone says, "Uldine," immediately there is the image, the love, and all the personality of my wife, the name of the one I love. "Uldine" is no different from any other name, but what the name implies is vastly different.

When someone says, "Billy, the Kid," I think of a Western villain. When they say, "Billy Graham," I think of a great evangelist. The name implies the individual. The mention of a name can cause physical reaction: fear, anger, jealousy, love, rage, or disgust. Would you name your child "Jezebel"? Probably not! Jezebel is just as good a name as Judy or Jane, but its implications are quite different.

Were I to go to a bank and write a note saying, "I want to borrow a million dollars" and sign my name "John R. Bisagno," the teller would look at the note, smile, and push it back through the window. My name is not worth a million dollars. But let me write the same note and at the bottom another person writes, "Okay by me," and signs "Bill Gates," I will get the money, not because I am coming in my merit but on the merit of one who is worth a million dollars and more.

What if I don't want the money for myself? I want it for Mr. Gates. He is my friend. I plan to spend all the money on him. It is for his sake, not mine, that I make my request. I still won't get the money because it is not for *his sake* but *in his name* that I ask. Yes, everything we do should be for the glory of God and the sake of His Son, but the biblical qualification for answered prayer is "in Jesus' name."

As kids, playing outside, one of my younger playmates would often tell his older brother he had to go in. Rarely would he respond until the powerful words were spoken, "*Mama said* we have to go in." Suddenly the message carried the authority the younger brother couldn't muster. It was now official. It came with the backing of the one in charge and the consequences attached to its disobedience.

Titles grant authority. The man with the title king is supreme over his domain. A president manages the affairs of a nation or a company. A general commands an army. The principal directs a school. A pastor leads a church. Their name is their authority.

When we pray in Jesus' name, we are not using it as a formulaic closing, hoping it will "seal the deal" to get what we prayed for. We are standing humbly in the authority of the only One who can come before the Father. Jesus is the signature on the check.

Privately and publicly, never be ashamed of the name of Jesus. Think what it means. Feel what it means. Imply it? Yes, but say it audibly for your benefit and those about you. *"Whatsoever ye shall ask in my name, that will I do, that the Father may be glorified in the Son"* (John 14:13 KJV).

God offers total access to His throne, all He is, all He can do because we come in His worthiness, in His will, and in His name. Praying in Jesus' name simply means to pray in the sum total of *all He is and wills*. And the key is that it ultimately brings glory to God.

> *For this reason God highly exalted Him and gave Him the name that is above every name, so that at the name of Jesus every knee will bow—of those who are in heaven and on earth and under the earth—and every tongue should confess that Jesus Christ is Lord, to the glory of God the Father. (Phil. 2:9–11)*

The Holy Spirit ransacked the alphabet to describe our lovely Lord Jesus. He called Him the Alpha, Bread, Christ, Daystar, Everlasting God, Friend of Friends, God of Grace, Healer, Incarnate Word, Justifier, King of Kings, Lord of

Lords, Master, Name above Every Name, Omnipotent, Prince of Peace, Quickener from the Dead, Resurrection, Savior, Truth, Unspeakable Gift, Very God of Very Gods, Water of Life, "X"press Image of God, Yesterday, Today, and Forever the Same, Zion's Hope, and Soon Coming Savior.

Praying recently at a public gathering, I was asked *not* to pray in Jesus' name lest I offend my Jewish brothers. "Then perhaps," I responded, "I can ask my Jewish brothers that they *do* pray in Jesus' name lest they offend me."

Never be ashamed of the sweetest name in heaven or earth.

Recently a judge ruled that a mother could not name her son "Messiah" because the baby could never become what the name implied.

The name of the baby Boy born in Bethlehem not only implied but was both who He was and would always be. And more!

CHAPTER 10

LISTEN TO HIM

The noise in our lives can drown out the voice of God. That is why it is important to find a quiet place to pray that we might sense His presence and hear His voice. Prayer is a conversation. We speak to God and He speaks to us. God is ready and willing to speak to us when we pray, but it can take a bit of effort to be sure we are not the only one talking.

Have you ever been far away from the noise of the city? No horns blasting, no cell phones ringing, no music blaring, no electronics humming—a place devoid of man-made noise, a place of silence. If you have, you know initially it seems so silent, but as you listen intently, you can hear the leaves rustling and even the bees buzzing. Leaves rustle and bees buzz in the city, but no one hears.

Sensing His presence is an "always thing." Listening to His voice is a "specific thing." Nothing *but* His voice. Waiting *for* God is waiting for Him to act. Waiting *on* God is waiting for Him to speak.

"Waiting on God" is not merely an abstract passing of time. It is a spiritual exercise at the end of your prayer, when, after having spoken to God, you wait for Him to speak to you.

And it isn't a loud, noisy voice. It's a deep, quiet impression in the soul. A thought. An idea. A soft whisper. And you just know it's His voice. *"My sheep hear My voice"* (John 10:27).

"Praying without ceasing" is sensing His presence *all through* the day as you do *other* things. "Waiting on God" is hearing His voice *early* in the day when listening is the *only* thing.

The Bible is filled with declarations of waiting on God:

Our soul waits for the LORD. (Ps. 33:20 NKJV)

I will wait on thy name. (Ps. 52:9 KJV)

My soul waiteth upon God. (Ps. 62:1 KJV)

I will wait on thy name. (Ps. 52:9 KJV)

These wait all upon thee. (Ps. 104:27 KJV)

They that wait upon the LORD shall renew
their strength. (Isa. 40:31 KJV)

Waiting upon God requires our entire being—all of our heart, soul, and mind. It is not drifting into daydreaming but an exercise that demands our keenest attention, and listening with all our heart. We must await Him patiently, not demanding He speak but humbly entreating His presence as we await His still small voice.

God seldom, if ever, speaks audibly or in our ears with a loud voice, but in our hearts with a voice so soft only we can hear it. But we know it's Him. We just know.

When we wait upon God, we do not wait *for* Him—He is already in our heart. We wait *on* Him to be fully formed within us and our desires and thoughts brought into total submission to His.

Psalm 46:10 (KJV) says, *"Be still, and know that I am God."* The Hebrew word for "be still" means "let go of your grip." We don't have to be in control and were never meant to be. By listening to the Lord and immediately responding, we allow Him to manifest Himself in our lives. Jesus only did what He saw His Father doing. *"Then Jesus replied, 'I assure you: The Son is not able to do anything on His own, but only what He sees the Father doing. For whatever the Father does, the Son also does these things in the same way'"* (John 5:19). He prayed and obeyed, even unto death.

> *I wait for Yahweh; I wait and put my hope in His word. I wait for the Lord more than watchmen for the morning—more than watchmen for the morning. (Ps. 130:5–6)*

"Speak, Lord, thy servants wait to hear," simply means, "Lord, *the answer is* **'Yes, what's the question?'**"

How much heartache and disappointment could we save ourselves if we learn to wait upon the Lord before we act? How many times have I said, "I wish I'd waited"?

Recently a friend said, "I've spent all my life thinking, *'Have I really done what God wanted me to do.'* But I've learned to give priority to what He wants me to do today and tomorrow."

The first difficulty you will inevitably encounter may seem a bit humorous, but if you pray very long, you will find to be a real problem. It is the problem of fatigue or drowsiness or just plain "being sleepy." When your mind is actively engaged in prayer, it is understandably not as likely to happen. When you empty it of your thoughts and desires and open it to the impression of God, you may have difficulty staying awake. You may wait before the Lord for an hour and never realize you were dozing a bit, and what seemed like connecting thoughts have actually come ten or twenty minutes apart.

If this happens, get up from your knees, lay down and sleep for an hour, splash cold water on your face, take a brisk walk, or do something to come into His presence at your brightest and best.

The second problem you will find is a rambling mind or wandering thoughts due to psychological association. Our minds are never empty. When they are not filled with conscious thoughts, the subconscious mind seems to take over, and we inevitably think about something. Many times as you wait before the Lord, a thought will come to mind. This thought will suggest another, then another, and then yet another, until you find yourself completely distracted from the Lord.

Suppose you are waiting on the Lord for His leadership in the purchase of a home. You've looked at many and are not certain which God would have you buy. As you wait upon the Lord for Him to impress you, naturally the image of some of the houses will appear on your mind.

As you think about it, you see yourself driving up in front of one of the houses. That reminds you that in back of your car is your fishing tackle, and you had planned to go fishing last Saturday. This reminds you it rained last Saturday and of a time when you were a child and went swimming in the rain, and so on. What's happened? Rather than waiting on God for direction about the house, you are off on a Saturday fishing trip or at the family swimming hole. One thing suggests another, and your mind wanders far from your original focus.

I have to fight distractions whenever I want to concentrate on God. Sometimes it helps to have a list of concerns. Looking at the paper helps me to stay focused a little better. The same is true of praying out loud. Speaking audibly to the "God Who is there" lessens my tendency to stray.

Frankly I can't imagine how God tolerates such insensitivity to His presence. We are kneeling before Him—are we not?—in the Great Throne Room of Heaven, speaking directly to Him. Yet we cannot keep from mentally leaving the room and chasing some silly thought.

In Gethsemane, Jesus asked the disciples to join Him as He prayed alone. Instead they fell asleep. He asked, "Could you not stay focused for one hour?" I can hear Him saying the same thing to me when I can't stay focused for five minutes.

If this occurs, center your mind on something physical. Personally, I see a great white throne with God seated upon it as I kneel before Him. Perhaps you will choose to picture an open Bible, a cross, or the face of Jesus as you envision

Him. This can serve as a lighthouse when your thoughts are lost at sea.

The third difficulty you will encounter is not so easily remedied. It is the problem of the subconscious mind. Psychologists suggest that virtually everything we have ever heard, read, seen, or thought is retained. Anything in the subconscious mind can surface. The devil will make great use of the subconscious mind and recall to your memory things you had completely forgotten and that should remain forgotten.

A young man seated on a plane casually glances through a magazine. He spends only a few seconds on every page, but each image is forever inscribed on his subconscious mind. Here is a picture of a baseball stadium in New York, a church in South America, a politician in London, a swimsuit model in Hollywood, an oil well in Texas. He thoughtlessly tosses the magazine and goes on to other things. That night he begins to pray and wait upon the Lord. What do you think is going to come out of his subconscious mind? The church? The politician? I think you know the answer.

When you pray, ask God to cleanse *even your subconscious* mind in the blood of Christ and keep forever *forgotten* that which is forever *forgiven*.

The fourth pitfall you will encounter is stray spirits. The Bible teaches that the devil and his emissaries are ever at work to destroy the effectual service of God's children.

> *Be serious! Be alert! Your adversary the Devil is prowling around like a roaring lion, looking for anyone he can devour. Resist him and be firm in the faith, knowing that the same sufferings are being experienced by your fellow believers throughout the world. (1 Pet. 5:8–9)*

Sometimes thoughts, ideas, and impressions will come into your mind, and you may wonder whether they are actually *from the Holy Spirit* or *from the devil.*

> *And no wonder! For Satan disguises himself as an angel of light. (2 Cor. 11:14)*

The word *Lucifer* means "light bearer" or "one who shines." While an attractive light, he is indeed a deceptive light. You will often have occasion to question whether that impression is from God or the devil.

But the ultimate Jesus-approved, devil-whoopin' safeguard against deception is the Word of God and the Shield of Faith. That which comes from the Spirit of God reflects the character of God and is consistent with the Word of God. If not, it is to be immediately rejected. It is that simple.

We must test the spirits to see whether or not they are from God (1 John 4:1–3), and the standard against which we test them is the Scripture. In this way Jesus withstood the temptation of Satan in the wilderness.

Our other defense is the Shield of Faith, *"Above all, taking the shield of faith with which you will be able to quench all the fiery darts of **the wicked one**"* (Eph. 6:16 NKJV, emphasis added).

"Above all" does not mean *most important of all*, but *over all* or *around all*. As you wait on the Lord, pray, "Lord, in faith I'm trusting You to shield my mind, that Satan may neither distract nor deceive. I trust You fully. I will act upon the impressions You give me and the thoughts You send me. I will believe they came from You."

In so doing, I have been neither deceived nor disappointed—ever.

Waiting on God allows His presence and person to be formed in you. You will learn to sense His voice, feel His heart, and pray His will.

Many years ago I bought a 1968 Ford F-100 pickup. It was several years out of warranty, and lots of things had gone wrong with it. One morning on my knees, I was quietly waiting on the Lord. Out of the quietness came a thought: *Maybe that truck's got a warranty,* and I wasn't even thinking about the truck.

After breakfast I dressed and drove to my office. On the way, I passed a Ford dealership and decided to check it out just for fun. A service writer greeted me in the service lane. And guess what? He was a member of my church. "Hi, Bro. John," he said. "What can I do for you today?"

I told him the story, and you won't believe what he said.

"Well, I've got good news for you. There have been so many problems with that particular truck that even though the warranty expired years ago, the Ford Motor Company just put a special one-time warranty on all of their 1968 F-100 pickups. They will fix everything wrong one time on one visit."

Thirty-eight hundred dollars worth of free repairs later, I drove out with a new air conditioner, new clutch, new radio, and more.

My preacher father-in-law, Dr. Paul Beck, was a saint. Early each morning he gave himself afresh to his Savior and finished with a time of waiting on God and prayed this prayer:

> I commit my mind to the shelter of the blood of Christ . . . that it shall not wander astray from God's will. I commit my thoughts to the efficacy of the blood of Christ . . . that they may be pure and edifying. My will . . . that it may be continually

His. I commit my desires . . . that they will be set upon no vain thing. My motives . . . that my eye might be single for His glory. My affections . . . that they might be set on things above. My imaginations . . . that I might be practical and spiritually minded. My personality . . . that it might witness for Him. I commit my body . . . the door to my heart . . . my entire being, to the protection of the blood of Christ that no harm shall come to me from the enemy. And then tonight, *"I will both lie down and sleep in peace, for You alone, Lord, make me live in safety" (Ps. 4:8).*

For more than sixty years these words from Andrew Murray's classic *Waiting on God* have helped make this the most precious part of my prayers.

Just be still before Him, and allow His Holy Spirit to waken and stir up in your soul the child-like disposition of absolute dependence and confident expectation. Wait upon God as a Living Being, as the Living God, who notices you, and is just longing to fill you with Himself. Wait on God till you know you have met Him; prayer will then become so different.

The special surrender to the Divine guidance in our seasons of prayer must cultivate, and be followed up by, the habitual looking upwards "all the day."

This is the blessedness of waiting upon God, that I confess the impotence of all my thoughts and efforts, and set myself still to bow my heart before Him in holy silence, and to trust Him to renew and strengthen His own work in me. "Let your heart take courage, all ye that wait on the Lord." Present it before Him as that wonderful part of your spiritual nature in which God reveals Himself, and by which you can know Him and know His will. Cultivate the greatest confidence that, though you cannot see into your heart, God is working there by His Holy Spirit. Let the heart wait at times in perfect silence and quiet; in its hidden depths God will work. Be sure of this, and just wait on Him.

In waiting upon God, our eye, looking up to Him, meets His looking down upon us.

If we desire to find a man whom we long to meet, we inquire where the places and the ways are where he is to be found. And He is actually in the silence.

In every true prayer there are two hearts in exercise. The one is your heart, with its little, dark, human thoughts of what you need and God can do.

The other is God's great heart, with its infinite, its divine purposes of blessing.

God is light, and is here shining on my heart. I have been so occupied with the rushlights of my thoughts and efforts. I have never opened the shutters to let His light in.

Waiting always centers on the character of the one on whom we wait. "But they that wait on the Lord, shall renew their strength; they shall mount up with wings as eagles. . . ." To wait is to soar into the very presence of God.

Even as the sunshine enters with its light and warmth, with its beauty and blessing, into every little blade of grass that rises upward out of the cold earth, so the Everlasting God meets, in the greatness and the tenderness of His love, each waiting child, to shine in his heart "the light of the knowledge of the glory of God in the face of Jesus."

At our first entrance into the school of waiting upon God, the heart is chiefly set upon the blessings which we wait for. God graciously uses our need and desire for help to educate us for something higher than we were thinking of. We were seeking gifts; He, the Giver, longs to give Himself and to satisfy the soul with His goodness. It is just for this reason that He often withholds the gifts, and that the time of waiting is made so long. He is all the time seeking to win the heart of His child for Himself.[1]

What an encouragement to know the Lord has been waiting on us! What confidence we have in His answer!

He waits that He may be gracious to us. *"Therefore the LORD is waiting to show you mercy, and is rising up to show you compassion, for the LORD is a just God. All who wait patiently for Him are happy"* (Isa. 30:18).

The Creator of the Universe wants to speak with us not because we have done good things but because He loves us. He waits patiently until we're ready to listen.

Let's not keep Him waiting.

SECTION 3

FURTHER

CHAPTER 11

PRAYING AGAINST DEMONIC POWERS

The Bible has much to say about the reality of spiritual warfare, an unseen battle raging about us, building strongholds in the mind—the ultimate goal.

Apparently when Lucifer rebelled in heaven in eternity past, one-third of the angels joined him, and when he was cast out, fell as well. Two passages suggest such a probability:

He said to them, "I watched Satan fall from heaven like a lightning flash." (Luke 10:18)

So the great dragon was thrown out—the ancient serpent, who is called the Devil and Satan, the one who deceives the whole world. He was thrown to earth, and his angels with him. (Rev. 12:9)

Lucifer became the devil. The fallen angels became demons. Satan came to the earth to continue his rebellion against the authority of God in the most fertile, sensitive, and important battlefield of all—the heart and mind of man, the master creation of God.

In the Garden of Eden, Satan tempted Eve with the original proposition, "You shall be as gods." The temptation to create a world in which he was himself God, and as such, at war with God, was too much. Succumbing to the forbidden fruit, Adam and Eve rebelled against the very God who had created them.

Born in each of us is a conflict. We are at once created in the image of God with a soul that longs for its Creator and shaped in iniquity, rebellious at the deepest core of our being. From conversion to glorification, the battle continues.

Satan could perpetrate no greater lie than that he does not exist, the idea of evil spirits laughable, and satanic warfare only a stumbling effort to personify everyday problems. Satanic warfare is real, the devil is alive and well, and demons attack and oppress (not possess) the people of God who live in a world under the control of one Paul calls, "The prince of the power of the air."

But in no New Testament passage are demonic spirits exorcised from believers.

We appeal for a sensible, balanced teaching on an issue critical to spiritual health and New Testament dynamism in the life of the believer, a true deliverance ministry. It must be neither ignored, denied, nor carried to the bizarre excesses we often see.

Balanced spiritual, mental, and emotional health does not emphasize the demonic, does not need a frame of reference for every problem, or personify every irritation that comes along. I once saw a woman attempt to cast "the washing machine demon" out of her Maytag.

The normal, mature Christian life is positive and rejoicing, focused on Christ, not on an obsession with demons. Every headache or anxious moment is not an attack of Satan and his evil spirits.

Luke, the beloved physician, who likely had keener insight into the relationship between the spirit, mind, and body than any New Testament writer, recorded seven instances when Jesus cast a spirit out of someone. In each, he makes it clear that it was an *evil* spirit by using the Greek word *acathartos*, meaning "unclean."

In Luke 13:12, Jesus healed a woman with a spirit of infirmity. This woman's problem was congenital *not* demonic. The expression "spirit of infirmity" is not preceded by the *acathartos*, an unclean spirit.

Every time it was an evil spirit or demon:

- The Gospels say it by using the word *acathartos*.
- Jesus addressed the demon, not the person.
- Jesus did not touch the demon-possessed person.

Here He addresses the woman and touches her. The woman possessed with the spirit of infirmity was not possessed with a demon. Everything that comes our way is not demonic.

The Bible makes it clear our troubles are from seven sources:

1. The lust of the flesh.
2. The lust of the eye.
3. The pride of life.
4. This present world system.
5. The devil.
6. God Himself, for our spiritual maturation.
7. No reason at all! Every problem doesn't have a spiritual dimension. Some things just happen.

Why did the bottom fall out of my grocery bag on the floor of the garage, breaking a quart of milk? Was it an act of Satan to tempt me to swear or an act of God to test my self-control? Probably neither. The juice simply fell out because the sack got wet!

How can we recognize the demonic?

Usually the Bible specifically says it is. But be careful to distinguish between what *is* and what merely *appears* to be, as in the case of the woman with a congenital disease.

The presence of severe and extreme behavior, uncontrolled anger, violence, hostility, and superhuman strength.

The external manifestation of an obvious and eerie sense of a presence within, often taking the form of another voice, changing facial countenance or severe distortion of personality.

Identifying a situation earlier in life in which one knowingly and willingly opened himself to satanic entrance for the sake of personal benefit or pleasure, thus creating a demonic stronghold which can only be overcome by prayer, the Word, and fasting.

Victory is clearly set forth in 2 Corinthians 10:3–5 (KJV), *"For though we walk in the flesh, we do not war after the flesh: (For the weapons of our warfare are not carnal, but mighty through God to the pulling down of strong holds;) Casting down imaginations, and every high thing that exalts itself against the knowledge of God, and bringing into captivity every thought to the obedience of Christ."*

A demonic stronghold can only continue to exist through satanic deception. We would expect no less from the father of lies who comes transformed as an angel of light. And the lie is—*The stronghold is bigger than God, undefeatable, unbreakable.*

But . . .

Satan is a liar

  The battle is winnable

    The demonic power defeatable

      The stronghold breakable

> *Finally, my brethren, be strong in the Lord and in the power of His might. Put on the whole armor of God, that you may be able to stand against the wiles of the devil. For we do not wrestle against flesh and blood, but against principalities, against powers, against the rulers of the darkness of this age, against spiritual hosts of wickedness in the heavenly places. Therefore take up the whole armor of God, that you may be able to withstand in the evil day, and having done all, to stand. Stand therefore, having girded your waist with truth, having put on the breastplate of righteousness, and having shod your feet with the preparation of the gospel of peace; above all, taking the shield of faith with which you will be able to quench all the fiery darts of the*

wicked one. And take the helmet of salvation, and the sword of the Spirit, which is the word of God; praying always with all prayer and supplication in the Spirit, being watchful to this end with all perseverance and supplication for all the saints. (Eph. 6:10–18 NKJV)

The key to overcoming *the lie* that perpetuates the stronghold is obviously *the truth.*

Jesus Christ is the truth, and the New Testament is the written record of Jesus. Satan's goal is a stronghold, and his weapon of choice is a lie. Darkness always crumbles before the Light and deception before the Truth.

The Word is the spiritual weapon of choice.

The entrance of Your words gives light. (Ps. 119:130 NKJV)

Your Word is truth. (John 17:17 NKJV)

When we read the Scripture, claim the promise, and pray the Word in positive faith, the battle is won. *"Take the helmet of salvation, and the sword of the Spirit, which is the word of God"* (Eph. 6:17 NKJV).

When we pray God's Word, we place within the hands of the Holy Spirit the *sword of truth* with which He destroys the stronghold the lie has established. Pray God's Word against demonic bondage in your life or another's. God's Word is undefeatable. It will accomplish that for which it was sent forth. Always.

> *So shall My word be that goes forth from My mouth; it shall not return to Me void, but it shall accomplish what I please, and it shall prosper in the thing for which I sent it. For you shall go out with joy, and be led out with peace; the mountains and the hills shall break forth into singing before you, and all the trees of the field shall clap their hands. (Isa. 55:11–12 NKJV)*

Read it, believe it, affirm it, claim it, pray it, and do it *positively* in *faith* believing. With the mountains and hills, you too will burst forth in songs of praise and, with the trees of the fields, clap your hands in joyous victory.

CHAPTER 12

PRAYING WITHOUT CEASING

The twelfth chapter of Acts records a specific historical event at a certain time in a particular place for one specific request: the release of the apostle Peter from confinement in a Roman prison.

> *Peter therefore was kept in prison: but prayer was made **without ceasing** of the church unto God for him. (Acts 12:5 KJV, emphasis added)*

First Thessalonians 5:17 (NKJV) is quite different. ***"Pray without ceasing,"*** is more an *attitude* than an *event*. More a *presence* than a *prayer*. More a *person* than a *petition*. It is a deep, unspeakable, precious, and gently settling sense of the abiding presence of Jesus.

Always there. Always sensitive. Never noisy. Neither blaring nor glaring.

Praying without ceasing is a holy fellowship that arises from our awareness of the *blessed assurance* that *Jesus is mine.* He is always with me, and my submission brings *perfect delight.* And it brings a sense of His presence every minute of every hour of every day. For all that we are to have all that He is, we abide in Him in joy or in pain.

It is a perpetual state of being in His presence, being aware of Him, sensing Him, listening to Him, that is as normal to us as breathing.

It's not an audible voice heard in the eardrums; it is a soft, warm light in the soul that assures and directs us, "Turn right, turn left, go here, act this way, do that." And much, much more.

Since I first fell in love with Uldine, like Willie Nelson's hit song, she is "Always on My Mind." I think about her every waking hour. Yet I do my work and all the many things I should be doing all day long.

So why can't I have *His* presence always on my mind? I can, when I love Him as I love her with all my heart.

Yield yourself to the Holy Spirit. Allow Him to surround your mind, control your thoughts, and flood your spirit. This maintains the awareness that God is always with you and prepares you to listen to His gentle voice anytime about anything and all in the sweetness of His abiding presence.

And it's all about God's Word. Those on the "milk of the Word" must start by getting off their "life is all about me" thing and on to an "it's all about living a life that pleases Him" thing. And it can only be done by those on the solid meat of the Word. How then do we keep our receptor open? *By saturating the mind, heart, and soul with God's Word.*

> *The revelation of Your words brings light and gives understanding to the inexperienced. (Ps. 119:130)*

> *Your word is a lamp for my feet and a light on my path. (Ps. 119:105)*

> *And whenever you turn to the right or to the left, your ears will hear this command behind you: "This is the way. Walk in it." (Isa. 30:21)*

F. B. Meyer called constant awareness *of* and fellowship *with* God "Practicing the Presence of God."

David said it beautifully as well:

> *I keep the LORD in mind always. Because He is at my right hand, I will not be shaken. (Ps. 16:8)*

*You reveal the path of life to me; in Your pres-
ence is abundant joy; in Your right hand are
eternal pleasures. (Ps. 16:11)*

Dr. Luke quotes King David in Acts 2:25–26: *"I saw the
Lord ever before me; because He is at my right hand, I will not
be shaken. Therefore my heart was glad."*

In his book *The Circle Maker,* Mark Batterson writes,
"Prayer isn't something we do with our eyes closed; we pray
with our eyes wide open. Prayer isn't a sentence that begins
with 'Dear Jesus' and ends with 'Amen.' In fact, the best
prayer doesn't even involve words at all; the best prayer is a
life well lived. All of life is meant to be a prayer, just as all
of life is meant to be an act of worship."[2]

The apostle Paul gently settles "Pray without ceasing"
into the context of two beautiful phrases of "joy" and
"gratitude." No explanation. No amplification. They may
well be the sweetest three verses of the epistles, enabling the
believer to experience everything He is to us as we walk the
path of life.

Rejoice evermore.
 Pray without ceasing.
  In every thing, give thanks.
   (1 Thess. 5:16–18 KJV)

In the midst of surrounding sin and sorrow, even then, *rejoice*. Even then, be *thankful* because you endlessly sense His presence.

- Rejoice evermore. (1 Thess. 5:16 KJV)
- In every thing give thanks. (1 Thess. 5:18 KJV)

Rejoicing and giving thanks *"in every thing"* does not mean *"for every thing."*

Sometimes there is sin. Sometimes there is unrighteousness, lying, adultery, murder. We do not give thanks *for* them; we give thanks even *in the midst* of them and rejoice—even *in spite* of them.

These two bookends, rejoicing and thanking, are possible because of the ceaseless presence of Jesus that lies between, *"pray without ceasing."*

Snuggled comfortably between the two—pray without ceasing—is more than a conversation; it is a connection.

To pray without ceasing doesn't mean to get on your knees 24/7 and stay there until God takes you home. It is the oxygen of the soul we seldom consciously inhale throughout the day. But it is always there because He is always there.

It is deeply breathing the air of His mind and heart, sensing Him in your spirit regardless of what your mind is thinking, your hands are doing, or your tongue is speaking.

And it doesn't create the constant presence of God; it makes you aware of it. Why would you ever want to leave it?

He is at the center of your mind, heart, and soul, your subconscious and conscious mind. No formula can define it. No scientist can explain it. But you know it. And *knowing* is the ultimate biblical expression of our union with the Son of God.

- *"Adam knew Eve his wife."* (Gen. 4:1 NKJV)
- *"How can these things be, seeing I know not a man?"* (Luke 1:34)
- *"Be still, and know that I am God."* (Ps. 46:10 NKJV)

Deep calls unto deep. His presence is always in the quiet sensing of His person—in you—about you—with you.

Elijah found God not in the wind, not in the earthquake, nor in the fire, but in His still, small voice.

There is no limit to the way God speaks to us. In His Word, in the heavens, in circumstances, in friends, in smiles, in memories, in whispers, in a touch. His presence is like a bubble around our mind, a cocoon around our heart.

Whisper His name—Emmanuel, God with us. Whisper His name, Jesus. Give Him the first hours of the morning. The earliest, the most quiet, the best. You'll know His presence every moment and every hour of the day.

That's praying without ceasing.

God is love, and there is no fear in love. Perfect love casts out fear. Relax within the veil. Be at peace. You can live as close to Him as you choose. He is saying, "Listen to Me." Your heart hears Him as your ears hear others. "Let me wash My love over you. Be still and breathe deeply of Me." Sit quietly in His presence. Early. First. And all throughout the day.

Hear Him speak to your soul:

• I'm already in your tomorrow. Every promised need I've already given you. *"I have given you every place where the sole of your foot treads, just as I promised Moses"* (Josh. 1:3).

• I will never forsake you. *"No one will be able to stand against you as long as you live. I will be with you, just as I was with Moses. I will not leave you or forsake you. Be strong and courageous, for you will distribute the land I swore to their fathers to give them as an inheritance. Above all, be strong and very courageous to carefully observe the whole instruction My servant Moses commanded you. Do not turn from it to the right or the left, so that you will have success wherever you go. This book of instruction must not depart from your mouth; you are to recite it day and night so that you may carefully observe everything written in it. For then you will prosper and succeed in whatever you do. Haven't I commanded you: be strong and courageous? Do not be afraid or discouraged, for the LORD your God is with you wherever you go"* (Josh. 1:5–9).

• You need not rush in fear. You can walk in the confidence of My presence. *"Even when I go through the darkest valley, I fear no danger, for You are with me; Your rod and Your staff—they comfort me"* (Ps. 23:4).

• I will keep you in perfect peace. *"You will keep the mind that is dependent on You in perfect peace, for it is trusting in You"* (Isa. 26:3).

• I will rejoice over you with love and singing. *"Yahweh your God is among you, a warrior who saves. He will rejoice over you with gladness. He will bring you quietness with His love. He will delight in you with shouts of joy"* (Zeph. 3:17).

• In My presence is fullness of joy. *"You reveal the path of life to me; in Your presence is abundant joy; in Your right hand are eternal pleasures"* (Ps. 16:11).

• Refresh yourself in My peace. In all circumstances know that I go before you. *"I have told you these things so that in Me you may have peace. You will have suffering in this world. Be courageous! I have conquered the world"* (John 16:33).

• Bring Me the sacrifice of your time. Sit quietly. Don't try to fathom My presence; enjoy it. *"The one who believes in Me, as the Scripture has said, will have streams of living water flow from deep within him"* (John 7:38).

• Know that I am continually with you, all the way home. *"Yet I am always with You; You hold my right hand.*

You guide me with Your counsel, and afterward You will take me up in glory" (Ps. 73:23–24).

Only last week as I penned these words, friends called to say that David Jeremiah had just told in a TV sermon the story from my earlier book on prayer about our daughter Melodye and her playhouse when she was only seven years old.

Having promised to build it just moments before, I was surprised to see her piling up her dolls and toys in one corner of the yard on a cold and snowy afternoon.

I had promised to build it.

She believed it.

She got it.

Across the years I have smiled as that story has become the most loved and remembered of my first *Power of Positive Praying.*

Perhaps this one may be as well.

Several years into retirement I repeatedly brought up the possibility of buying a puppy. Again. And again. To no avail.

"I never had a dog," Uldine said.

"Honey," I said, "we've had lots of dogs."

"But those were the kids' dogs. I never had one of my own."

"NEVER?" I said.

"Well," she replied, "I did have a little puppy when I was twelve that I found on the street. But after three days, Daddy said we couldn't afford him so I had to take him to the pound."

"That settles it," I said. "We're going puppy hunting. Tomorrow!"

We found a beautiful, six-week-old Havanese Poodle and named her Andi. Please don't think me sacrilegious. I speak from my heart, not my theological commentaries, but we call her our "Jesus puppy."

She has truly taught us so much about how He loves us and wants us to love Him back.

She doesn't want anything. No questions. No complaints. No requests. No demands. She just wants to be close to us. All day, everywhere, anywhere, all the time. When we sit down, she gets on the top of the highest pillow in the room, as near to our face as possible. When we walk, she follows our every step. When we sit, she curls up in our lap 100 percent of the time. I think her gift is sleeping—many hours a day. And it only makes us love her more.

When we take a trip, Andi has no idea where she's going or what's going to happen, and she couldn't care less. She is just happy to be with us.

When I was about ten years old, my mother wrote a song about our little dog. Uldine and I sing it to Andi just about every night.

You're a little beggar
That's what you are
Mommy's little beggar
Eyes are like stars
You beg me to love you
You beg for a pat
You beg to be petted
And all such as that

Funny little puppy
Wants to be fed
Now you're nearly tuckered
Begging for bed
You beg all day
But more than pay
With love for all I've done
For you're the sweetest little beggar
'neath the sun

Every morning go to Him. Don't rush there; relax there.

Thank Him.

Praise Him.

Tell Him.

Ask Him.

Honor Him.

Listen to Him.

Then just curl up in His lap, nice and cozy, and enjoy the pats.

And you won't even have to beg.

CHAPTER 13

PRAYING THE LORD'S PRAYER

Since Moses and Jesus walked the earth, the Ten Commandments and the Lord's Prayer have blessed the human race. The commands of God to man—the prayer of man to God. The Ten Commandments consists of 297 words. The Lord's Prayer of 56.

The Ten Commandments are the fabric of civilization; the Lord's Prayer, the foundational creed of the Kingdom. The Lord's Prayer was offered by apostles and laymen before the church was organized. It is the keystone of Christian prayer and serves as the catalyst and blueprint for all prayer.

Adam and Eve were genetically encoded from the beginning to worship and pray. Prayer is the way God has chosen for us to communicate with Him, beyond "man to man" to "man to God."

What we commonly call the *Lord's Prayer* is really the *Model Prayer*—how Jesus taught us to pray. The real Lord's Prayer, the most insightful and passionate He ever prayed, comprises the entire seventeenth chapter of John.

People universally call the Model Prayer, the Lord's Prayer. For the sake of familiarity, we shall do so as well.

In the tradition of each rabbinical school, students were taught to pray in a unique manner. Anywhere they prayed, people immediately recognized the school from which they came. Against this backdrop, the disciples came to Jesus and asked that they too might have a prayer that others might recognize them as His disciples.

> *Now it came to pass, as He was praying in a certain place, when He ceased, that one of His disciples said to Him, "Lord, teach us to pray, as John also taught his disciples." (Luke 11:1 NKJV)*

The Lord's Prayer is like a beautiful play in three acts.

Act 1 of the prayer is *"Our Father which art in heaven, Hallowed be thy name. Thy kingdom come. Thy will be done in earth, as it is in heaven."* Everything focuses on God. Nothing is said about man, the family, or the disciples—only the Father, His name, His Kingdom, and His will.

The pronoun *our* is used throughout the Lord's Prayer. As His children we have a distinct relationship with God "our" Father and a distinct responsibility to "our" fellow-man. There is no mention of the word *I* or *me* or *mine*; it is always *our*. We pray for ourselves but also *for* and *with* the family of God. As brothers and sisters in Christ, we are part of the family of God. As you pray, think of your brothers and sisters.

There never was a Sunday morning staff prayer meeting that we didn't name many of the churches in Houston and pray for them.

Do we realize how great is the family of God? I have spent some wonderful Sunday mornings in thatch huts in Africa and stilt houses in South America. I have stood in the mud in India with God's people, waiting for a truck to distribute food that they might live another day. I often think of them and many others when I pray. The Lord's Prayer first gives attention to God and then to the family of God. In rightly positioning these two things, our personal needs fall into place.

Perhaps the two most often heard prayers in heaven are "Why me?" and "Give me." But Jesus taught that our requests are to be set in context of focus on Him. The Lord's Prayer begins and ends with attention on God Himself, His Kingdom, His glory!

The second word in Act 1 is *Father*. Abba/Father was used by the youngest child in Israel who sat on his daddy's knee and put his chubby little hands on his face, calling him the most endearing, intimate word, *Abba*. The nearest translation we have in English is *daddy*. That almost sounds sacrilegious, doesn't it? But it is the only word in the English language that comes close to what *Abba* means. Jesus would have us think of God as the most tender, caring, understanding, loving Father of all.

A Roman emperor was returning from battle riding the lead chariot in the victory parade. Suddenly a little boy jumped down from the reviewing stand, ran between the legs of the guard, and climbed into the chariot. The guard picked him up, "Son, you can't come up here. He's the Emperor." The little boy said, "But he's *my* daddy."

God wants us to think of Him like that.

But intimacy must not breed familiarity and ultimately, contempt. Immediately Jesus adds, "Hallowed be Thy name." *Hallowed* means "holy, sanctified, set apart," which in turn means "unique." And remember there are no degrees of uniqueness. Our God is not one of a kind. He is the *Only One*. God is not like anyone else or anything else; therefore, His name is not like any other name.

The Lord's Day is not like any other day; it is a hallowed day. The Bible is not like any other book; it is a hallowed book, as is our God and His name. *"Hallowed be thy name."*

Immediately after our familiarity with a loving Abba, heavenly Father, Jesus teaches us to pray, *"Hallowed be thy name."*

So holy was God's name to Jewish scribes, they destroyed their pen each time they wrote it and used another to continue writing. We are not ready to rightly relate to others until we first rightly position God in our hearts.

Jesus goes on to say, *"Thy kingdom come"*—period. *"Thy will be done in earth as it is in heaven"*—period. These are separate sentences, using a common device of the Greek to emphasize by saying essentially the same thing twice.

The kingdom of God is a place where the will of the King is done.

There are three senses of the kingdom of heaven. The kingdom of God *was* in heaven before Satan's rebellion, *is now* in our hearts through Christ, and *will be* on earth during His millennial reign and throughout eternity in the new heaven and new earth.

The Lord's Prayer is set in the Sermon on the Mount—the constitution of the Kingdom. The Beatitudes are the preamble. Nine times it says *blessed*, meaning "happy." The purpose of the Kingdom is to enable people to be happy by loving the King and doing His will.

Act 2 of the Lord's Prayer addresses our personal needs. *"Give us this day our daily bread."* What does Jesus mean by *"our daily bread"*? Some suggest the Eucharist, the Lord's Supper, or Communion. That is not likely. Others suggest Jesus is talking about Himself, and that is certainly a beautiful thought, for He is indeed our Daily Bread. And we, like the Israelites, daily gather the manna.

But Jesus likely refers to our physical food. Certainly He wants us to be constantly aware that both spiritual and physical daily bread come from Him. Before the loaf was the flour; before the flour, the mill; before the mill, the wheat, the rain, and the sun; before the sun, the Father Himself.

It is possible to live your entire life, never pray this prayer, and have plenty to eat. But it is not likely we will become the children our Father wants us to be until we first focus on the One who supplies even our most basic needs.

"Forgive us our trespasses." This word has been interchangeably interpreted "trespasses," "sins," and "debts." All of which are good translations. There are four Greek words translated "sin" in the New Testament.

1. *Parabasis* means "to step across the line."
2. *Paratoma* means "to accidentally slip across the line."

3. *Anomia* means "deliberate rebellion."

4. *Ophelama* means "to repay a debt."

The word Jesus uses here, *ophelama*, teaches us we must forgive the debt others owe us, that God might forgive the debt we owe Him.

That does not mean God's gracious forgiveness is conditioned on some human work I do. It does mean, if I have not the humility to forgive others, I will never have the humility to recognize I too need the forgiveness of God.

Then Jesus says, *"Lead us not into temptation, but deliver us from evil."* Are we to understand we must ask God, who cannot be tempted with evil, not to lead us into sin? No. The Greek word translated "temptation" here is the word *paradxi*, which means "trial." We are to pray, "Lord, don't let it get too hard for me. Remember I'm human. Don't put more trial on me than by Your grace I can bear."

"And keep me from evil." The word *evil* means "the Evil One." There are three Greek words that may be translated "evil one." This one means "the one who accuses me." When I get in trouble, the devil loves to say, "It's because of something bad he did." So Jesus teaches us to pray the Evil One will be silenced and God will be trusted that He alone leads us into situations that test us and try us, for our good, by His grace, and for His glory.

Pray for the past, *"Forgive us our debts."* Pray for today, *"Give us our daily bread."* Pray for tomorrow, *"Lead us not into temptation."* That pretty well sums it up.

Like two bookends, Act 3 returns our focus to the Lord. *"For thine is the kingdom, and the power, and the glory, for ever."* This phrase was at the end of every Jewish prayer, a benediction or closing like, "In Jesus' name, Amen."

Begin with focus on God and His Kingdom, review the panorama of our human need, and close by bringing Him again into focus.

"Lord, it's Your Kingdom, and it's up to You to sustain me as a citizen of Your Kingdom. It's Your power that helps me stand in it, and it's for Your glory that I do." It is a beautiful prayer of dependence on the Father that first positions the Lord of the Kingdom and ourselves as citizens in it.

Let me offer three suggestions:

1. Pray the Lord's Prayer often. To my heart, it is the sweetest, most personal and reverent prayer in the world.

2. Pray it prayerfully and thoughtfully. Not just words, not just by rote, but with all the delight and passion of your soul.

3. Beyond its words, pray with your words. The Lord's Prayer is both a prayer and a prayer guide, a prayer to pray and *how* to pray. Embellish and personalize every word and every phrase, and make it your own.

CHAPTER 14

PRAYING FOR REVIVAL

Unless true spiritual awakening has come to America, by the time you read this in 2015 and beyond, these numbers will be worse:

- 72 percent of adults (ages eighteen to twenty-eight) were aborted in the womb, have had an abortion, are in the penitentiary, are out on parole, are addicted to drugs or alcohol, have attempted suicide, or are in the occult.
- 81 percent of young adults cohabitate.
- 58 percent of marriages end in divorce.
- Homosexuality is celebrated.
- Gay marriage is legal in eighteen states.
- The fastest growing religion in America is Islam. The second is Mormonism. The third is the occult. The fourth is Christianity.

- More churches closed in America last year than any year in history.
- Fifteen hundred men and women leave the ministry every month.
- Only one in five seminary graduates is still in ministry eight years after graduation.
- Persecution of Christians increases.
- Terrorism threatens.
- Martyrdom is on the horizon.

America has no tomorrow, no future, and no hope, except for true, old-fashioned, heaven-sent revival. No nation has gone where we have gone and escaped the judgment of God. We shall not be the first.

Second Chronicles 7:14 (NKJV) gives God's eternal, absolute, unchanging formula for revival. *"If My people who are called by My name will humble themselves, and pray and seek My face, and turn from their wicked ways, then I will hear from heaven, and will forgive their sin and heal their land"* (emphasis added).

God does not say, "If the politicians, if the pornographers, if the drug pushers, or gang lords." He says, "If My people." We're the cause and we're the cure.

Jesus said, "You're the salt of the earth." Salt preserves. If the meat of society has spoiled, it is because the salt has lost its savor. Salt is bitter to society. Salt bites. Salt challenges and salt changes. The preaching of the Cross and living it out will always be an offense to society, but without it, society will rot and die. And it has.

Rather than changing society, I fear "political correctness" has changed us. Being friendly to sinners has become friendly to their sin in too many pulpits. Preaching against the sins of society breaks open the rocky soil so the gospel may infuse the rock and melt it.

Humble yourself. If your pastor walks in and out of the pulpit like a rock star, pray for him. And the same goes for us. Hide yourself as far as possible from the limelight. Every revival in history has begun, not in the hearts of the rich and famous but in the broken, humble, hidden, *and unlikely.* As you go before the Lord and pray for revival, pray that no one will ever know your name but everyone will know His.

Pray that your pastor will cry out against sin and plead for brokenness and repentance from the pulpit. And pray for brokenness and burden in the pulpit of your own heart. In both pulpits we stand, as did men in the pulpit of the bow of great ships, willingly tied there at the peril of our lives, crying aloud with warnings of rocks in the water that can sink the ship. In the name of Jesus, speak out and speak up. Without God's people *being* God's people, we are doomed.

Seek the face of God. Pray that God will make Himself your passion. To seek His face in praying for revival, is to pray for the total abandonment of your will to His.

His will. His honor. His name. His Kingdom. His land.

Pray, "Lord, with all the sincerity of my soul, I ask, 'What do You want of me?' Speak Lord; Thy servant waits to hear. I will do anything You tell me. Go anywhere You send me. Forfeit anything You ask me. Be anything You want of me."

> *All to Jesus I surrender;*
> *All to him I freely give;*
> *I will ever love and trust him,*
> *In his presence daily live.*
> *—J. W. Van Deventer*

Turn from your wicked ways. What we see as little things, God sees as big. Our little white lies are big black lies to Him. Our racial slurs crush His spirit. Our sins of omission stop His hand. No praying, no witnessing, no giving, no forgiving paralyze His plan. We are His chosen vessels, His instruments, His body, His hands and feet. He can choose to do anything He wishes, and what He has chosen to do is work through us. Pray that He will forgive our sins and heal our land.

God always has mercy upon a remorseful people, mourning over their sins with a yearning to change.

America is sick. Politicians, educators, financiers, intellectuals, social commentators have not a clue how to make her well again. You do. God just told you. God promised you. He has done it before. You've read it countless times. Did it go right over your head? It's in your hands. We're not waiting for Him. *He is waiting for us.*

Don't say, "Why doesn't God do something?" God is saying, *"Why don't you do something?"*

His promise to heal our land is more than a promise. It's a law.

We see physical law enacted every day in the natural world. An apple separates from a tree and falls downward. A glass of water chilled to thirty-two degrees becomes ice.

When God enacts a situation, it is more than a divine promise. It is a spiritual law. He is not simply saying, "If you lower the temperature to thirty-two degrees, as a reward I promise to give you ice."

He is saying, "There will be ice." Meet My conditions— the law of revival is engaged—*the land is healed.*

And He always requires that we act first.

"If you will, I will."

When you pray for revival, don't try to direct God in the how, who, where, and when. *Every great awakening in the history of the church was a surprise.* Each began with an unlikely, unexpected person. Never by the plan or official decree of the establishment. In AD 33, a handful of people prayed in an upper room, and *suddenly* there came a sound from heaven like a mighty rushing wind.

The revival under Samuel began in the heart of a concerned woman at least a generation before it broke out. Don't give up.

Three armies were coming toward Jehoshophat. He proclaimed a fast, prayed, and sang praises to the Lord in the beauty of holiness.

God smote the armies. Pray.

Keep on asking. Keep on seeking. Keep on praying. Don't quit. Let prayer be the priority of your life. And tell your pastor you are willing to do anything to help him promote *the explicit agreement and visible union of the churches of your area for extraordinary revival.*

God has never once resisted the visible, united, passionate prayer of His people.

> *After a long time, the king of Egypt died. The Israelites groaned because of their difficult labor, and they cried out; and their cry for help ascended to God because of the difficult labor. (Exod. 2:23)*

> *"When we cried out to the LORD, He heard our voice, sent an angel, and brought us out*

of Egypt. Now look, we are in Kadesh, a city on the border of your territory." (Num. 20:16)

"When Jacob went to Egypt, your ancestors cried out to the LORD, and He sent them Moses and Aaron, who led your ancestors out of Egypt and settled them in this place." (1 Sam. 12:8)

They received help against these enemies because they cried out to God in battle, and the Hagrites and all their allies were handed over to them. He granted their request because they trusted in Him. (1 Chron. 5:20)

Then they cried out to the LORD in their trouble; He rescued them from their distress. (Ps. 107:6)

Announce a sacred fast; proclaim an assembly! Gather the elders and all the residents of the land at the house of the LORD your God, and cry out to the LORD. (Joel 1:14)

Pray, pray, pray. God has often sent spiritual awakening to His people and only waits for us to do so again.

- Elijah
- Isaiah

- Jehoshophat
- Elisha
- Haggai
- Pentecost
- The First Great Awakening
- The Second Great Awakening
- The Welsh Revival
- The Azusa Street Revival
- The Asbury Revival
- The Howard Payne University Revival
- The Jesus Movement

Old Testament revival started *from the top down.* A prophet, one person in one body preached, the people responded in repentance. Since New Testament days, revival has started mostly *from the people up.* Unofficial, unexpected, unlikely.

Often with students. *Always with prayer.* **Always a surprise.**

What happened in the New Testament? At Calvary Christ died for His bride the church. At Pentecost, the Holy Spirit of Christ birthed the church.

Since Pentecost, He moves through *a new body, a greater body, millions of people, His bride, the church.* Jesus said in the coming of His Holy Spirit, "These works shall you do—**and greater.**"

The potential for world-impacting revival is even greater this side of Pentecost. The way up is down. The way to live is to die. The way to revival is denial. Self, sin, pleasure, food, time. Anything. Everything.

Fast. Repent. Seek. *And pray.*

The real question is, "If prayer is the key, what will it take for us to begin to plead with God for revival?"

1. A conviction that our nation is broken and it's something we cannot fix.
2. A concert of prayer by Christians who are more interested in talking together to God than debating theological differences.
3. A company of preachers who stand as did the Old Testament prophets and declare what God says. And it doesn't have to be a large number. Sometimes one is enough.

Something special will happen when God removes the blindness from the eyes of His children. We must see the truth; we are the problem and we are the solution. It's still about *"if My people."*

If your eyes are open, your knees should be down until He opens more eyes and we see more knees down.

Revival is the tool. Spiritual awakening is the goal. A healed land is the result. *Pray.*

CHAPTER 15

PRAYING FOR THE LOST

Sadly, the evangelistic fervor of the church seems to have been lost. Virtually no revivals, evangelistic sermons, or invitations, and conversions perpetually declining.

Theological debate has replaced evangelism at center stage of Southern Baptist life and many other evangelical denominations. It has been a progressive, theological downward spiral, which began with the question, "Did Christ die for the sins of the whole world?"

Clearly the answer is "Yes."

> *He Himself is the propitiation for our sins, and not only for ours, but also for those of **the whole world**. (1 John 2:2, emphasis added)*

> *For there is one God and one mediator between God and humanity, Christ Jesus, Himself human, who gave Himself—**a ransom for all**, a testimony at the proper time. (1 Tim. 2:5–6, emphasis added)*

Now the issue has devolved into the question, "Do we coerce and manipulate someone when we lead them to pray the Sinner's Prayer to be saved?"

The next issue may well be virtually no emphasis on asking sinners to do anything at all, neither hear our witness, nor respond to the gospel.

Clearly we should pray for the salvation of the lost. The Bible teaches it.

> *Ask of Me, and I will make the nations Your inheritance and the ends of the earth Your possession. (Ps. 2:8)*

> *Brothers, my heart's desire and prayer to God concerning them is for their salvation! (Rom. 10:1)*

Logic dictates it.

First of all, then, I urge that petitions, prayers, intercessions, and thanksgivings be made for everyone. (1 Tim. 2:1)

If we are to intercede for *all* men, that includes lost men. And for what should we pray if not that they should become saved men.

Scripture emphasizes it. At the seaside, Jesus gave the disciples the gospel. Behind closed doors He gave them the power of the Holy Spirit to make their witness of it effective. Then He gave them the command to take it to the lost and warned them of the seriousness of not doing so.

Jesus said to them again, "Peace to you! As the Father has sent Me, I also send you." After saying this, He breathed on them and said, "Receive the Holy Spirit. If you forgive the sins of any, they are forgiven them; if you retain the sins of any, they are retained." (John 20:21–23)

Jesus was not saying, as Catholicism suggests, that one may forgive the sins of another. He was saying, "If you don't witness, you are responsible for retaining men in their sin because you did not go in the power I gave you and announce the terms of the gospel *under which* sin may be remitted."

Is there any connection between prayer and evangelism? A ten-day prayer meeting in the Upper Room nailed that at Pentecost.

There's a lot I *don't know* about the relationship between prayer and the power of God that brings men to Jesus Christ. But let me tell you what I do know.

In thirteen years as a full-time evangelist, thirty-five as a pastor, and fifteen in retirement, I have preached about seven hundred evangelistic crusades, five hundred in churches, and two hundred in stadiums.

In each, I tried to spend one to two hours in prayer every afternoon before I preached that evening. Sometimes I didn't. Most of the time, I did. I can absolutely tell you that without exception there was a direct relationship between the amount of time I spent on my knees each afternoon and the number of people who walked the aisles to accept Christ as their Savior that night.

In the first revival of my ministry in Belfast, Ireland, three hundred and sixty people were saved in Immanuel Baptist Church. The night before it began, eighty of us prayed all night.

The last evening of a great citywide crusade in Alexandria, Louisiana, over seven hundred persons, among them 165 adult men, accepted Christ as Savior. The night before three hundred men met together and prayed all night for the service.

In Delmar Stadium in Houston, I preached on "What to do if you miss the rapture." I spent the entire night before in prayer. One hundred forty-seven people began running forward before I had even finished the sermon.

Pastor Ronnie Floyd recounts forty days of prayer and fasting by his church for one thousand persons to be saved during a seven-day evangelistic crusade. The first service was cancelled due to a huge snowstorm. In faith, they added back not one but two nights to the crusade. In the eight nights, there were not one thousand conversions; there were two thousand six hundred!

- Jonathan Edwards prayed twelve to fourteen hours every time he preached "Sinners in the Hands of an Angry God," and men screamed aloud and clung to the pillars of the church for fear they would slide into hell.
- Edward Peyson prayed until his knees wore grooves in the floor.

- David Brainerd prayed until the snow melted beneath him.
- *And they moved the hand of God.*

Pray for the lost? Of course! God's Word teaches it. History proves it. Experience validates it. Passion dictates it. Common sense affirms it.

If my grandchildren are in a burning house, I'm not going to stand on the front porch and debate the theory of spontaneous combustion. I'm going to risk my life and rush in and try to save them.

Your son is addicted to drugs. Your daughter is cohabitating. Your husband is lost. How in heaven's name can you not plead with God in prayer for them?

Our nation is perishing. Society is deteriorating. Families are imploding. Jesus is the only answer. Men need Christ. Love them. Engage them. Witness to them. *Pray for them.* And *win* them.

God's revelation of His election was intended to remove the pressure from our witness, not the passion.

That the elect are waiting to be found should heighten our zeal to find them, not lessen it.

CHAPTER 16

PRAYER AND FASTING

Glorious wonders in prayer abound.

The wonder that we may pray at all. How marvelous that our Father would not only allow but actually urge our petitions. The wonder that we may pray naturally and simply. Nice-sounding phrases and sophisticated theology give way to speaking to God as a child to his father. The wonder that we may pray specifically. Vague and general prayers receive only vague and general answers. The wonder that we may pray anywhere. *"Therefore, I want the men in every place to pray, lifting up holy hands without anger or argument"* (1 Tim. 2:8).

The wonder that we may pray all the time. He who never slumbers nor sleeps can't wait to hear the voices of His children. The wonder that we may pray about everything. Nothing is of disinterest to God. If it's important to us, it is important to our heavenly Father. *"Don't worry about anything, but in everything, through prayer and petition with thanksgiving, let your requests be made known to God"* (Phil. 4:6).

The wonder that we may pray boldly. We are invited to enter the throne room boldly and confidently. *"Therefore let us approach the throne of grace with boldness, so that we may receive mercy and find grace to help us at the proper time"* (Heb. 4:16).

The wonder that no problem is too difficult for God. The plain fact is, however, that there are degrees of difficulty that seem to require different degrees of power. Jesus told the powerless disciples who were unable to heal a severely mentally challenged boy, *"This kind does not come out except by prayer and fasting"* (Matt. 17:21, emphasis added).

For years I believed fasting was something you did because you so passionately longed to see God do some particular thing you simply lost your appetite. Today I have come to understand while this may indeed be the ideal, the reality is we fast because we are willing to pay any price to move the hand of God.

In fasting we're not doing some "self-flagellation" to pressure God to answer. We're saying to ourselves and our Lord that we are subjecting all things, even our appetite, to the main thing—giving total attention to our Father.

Pastor Ronnie Floyd writes, "To fast means to deny ourselves what is common, normal, necessary, and desirable—food—for a period of time, so that our minds may become sharp, our hearts softened, and our spirits receptive to what God has to say to us. The price is great, but worth it. Why? God promises to fill the void that the absence of food creates; He will pour out His blessings and sate us in a way that food neither can nor will."[3]

Fasting is not easy. But it's worth it. And with *His* help, you *can do it.*

> *Now this is what the* LORD *says—the One who created you, Jacob, and the One who formed you, Israel—"Do not fear, for I have redeemed you; I have called you by your name; you are Mine. I will be with you when you pass through the waters, and when you pass through the rivers, they will not overwhelm you. You will not be scorched when you walk through the fire, and the flame will not burn you." (Isa. 43:1–2)*

> *I am able to do all things through Him who strengthens me. (Phil. 4:13)*

And we must be desperate.

Do we want something to happen desperately enough? If so, we must pay the price and do what it takes. How badly do you really want it? Jehoshaphat wanted God more than food or anything.

> *After this, the Moabites and Ammonites, together with some of the Meunites, came to fight against Jehoshaphat. People came and told Jehoshaphat, "A vast number from beyond the Dead Sea and from Edom has come to fight against you; they are already in Hazazon-tamar" (that is, En-gedi). Jehoshaphat was afraid, and he resolved to seek the LORD. Then he proclaimed a fast for all Judah. (2 Chron. 20:1–3)*

Fasting humbles us and exalts Him.

Fasting satisfies the heart more on Living Bread than human bread.

Fasting turns our focus to spiritual goals. I love the phrase "God's chosen fast."

> ***Isn't the fast I choose:*** *To break the chains of wickedness, to untie the ropes of the yoke, to set the oppressed free, and to tear off every yoke? Is it not to share your bread with the hungry, to bring the poor and homeless into your house,*

*to clothe the naked when you see him, and not to ignore your own flesh and blood? Then your light will appear like the dawn, and your recovery will come quickly. Your righteousness will go before you, and the LORD's glory will be your rear guard. **At that time, when you call, the LORD will answer; when you cry out, He will say, "Here I am." If you get rid of the yoke among you, the finger-pointing and malicious speaking.** (Isa. 58:6–9, emphasis added)*

As you fast, focus not primarily on that for which you are fasting, focus on Him. And that means privately. Fast in such a way that *no one will ever know* you're doing so.

Whenever you fast, don't be sad-faced like the hypocrites. For they make their faces unattractive so their fasting is obvious to people. I assure you: They've got their reward! (Matt. 6:16)

My friend Roger Patterson graciously shared his journey in fasting:

1. **Praying and fasting exposes my sinfulness.** When I fast, my flesh can dominate my thinking. I have struggled with my weight since I was a kid, and this year told the

church I was going to lose fifty pounds. Stuck on dead center halfway to my goal, I got stressed and guess what? I started to eat—and eat. For the first time, I saw how much God was letting me see the predominance of the flesh in my life. In seasons of fasting and prayer, God shows me just how much I need Him. Unless I had set aside time to fast and pray, I would never have realized how easily I have allowed myself to become desensitized to the sin in my own heart.

2. **Prayer and fasting turn cloudiness to clarity.** My wife and I were considering selling our home to be closer to our church. We put our house on the market for months, showed it over forty times and received only one, ridiculously low offer. I decided to fast and pray. It took ten days for me to understand what God wanted me to hear.

During the process I came to Proverbs 19:2, *"It is not good to have zeal without knowledge, nor to be hasty and miss the way"* (NIV). Only in fasting did I learn that He graciously brings confusion and cloudiness into our lives to get us to seek Him. My heavenly Father wasn't against our move; the timing just wasn't right. The cloudiness that initiated that ten-day fast turned to clarity that it was the right move but the wrong time. We sold the house for a much better price. Later.

3. **Prayer and fasting exposes my call to stewardship.** I deeply long not to be the "one talent" steward, burying my gifts and displeasing the Giver. When I fast and pray about the "over and above" God would have me give from my heart, from my family, from my church, I have seen spiritual breakthrough that set my foot in the Promised Land. Ministry, missions, and mercy to our city are three specific areas where God has clearly revealed His will to me through prayer and fasting.

4. **Prayer and fasting position me for God's surprises.** One of the first surprises in this season of fasting was the opportunity to make this contribution to Dr. Bisagno's book you are reading. Having lunch to discuss something completely unrelated, I mistakenly scheduled our time together during my weekly Monday fast. So I got to watch him eat fried redfish while I sipped iced tea. This opened the door to discuss this very topic and the invitation to make a contribution. What a surprise!

During my seasons of prayer and fasting, many doors have swung open wide. Possibilities have developed that could only be the hand of God. My journey of weekly prayer and fasting has been filled with surprises, excitement, and adventure.

Don't be surprised when you set yourself apart for the Lord and He gives you some really special opportunities both to bless and to be blessed.

CHAPTER 17

AGREEING IN PRAYER

Matthew 18:19 is a surprise verse. *"Again, I assure you: If two of you on earth agree about any matter that you pray for, it will be done for you by My Father in heaven."*

Agreeing in prayer can be a powerful blessing. And it is a joy. Praying together. Believing together. Receiving together. If two or three agreeing can do great things, think what a dozen did when He called His disciples. Or 120 at Pentecost. It was a prayer meeting in the Upper Room that *birthed* the church at Pentecost. And it was a prayer meeting *by* the church that got its preacher out of prison.

Two or three, in a little bitty church, can do just as much as two or three thousand in a great big church. With God there are no small churches or large churches, just powerful churches waiting to happen.

Go to church.

Be the church.

Be one.

Worship as one.

Pray as one.

Agree as one.

Receive as one.

God's people in one accord can do anything. *"When we cried out to the Lord, He heard our voice, sent an angel, and brought us out of Egypt. Now look, we are in Kadesh, a city on the border of your territory"* (Num. 20:16).

> *They received help against these enemies because they cried out to God in battle, and the Hagrites and all their allies were handed over to them. He granted their request because they trusted in Him. (1 Chron. 5:20)*

Before Pentecost, the people agreed in prayer.

> *When they arrived, they went to the room upstairs where they were staying: Peter, John, James, Andrew, Philip, Thomas, Bartholomew, Matthew, James the son of Alphaeus, Simon the Zealot, and Judas the son of James. All these were continually united in prayer, along*

*with the women, including Mary the mother
of Jesus, and His brothers. (Acts 1:13–14)*

Ten days later—*wow!*

Before its preacher got out of jail, the church prayed all night for his release. *"So Peter was kept in prison, but prayer was being made earnestly to God for him by the church"* (Acts 12:5). By this time, the Jerusalem church was very large.

And Jesus was explicitly clear that two or three could have done the same thing.

At the moment of need, we may not be in God's will. We may not be that "righteous man" or "righteous woman," struggling with a temptation or an addiction. We may be trying to come out of some sin, and our rebellious heart cannot move heaven.

But if a person who loves the Lord and is serving Him comes to God on our behalf, our God hears. He is touched when those who love Him are so moved with compassion for another that they come alongside the struggler to help him find his way. The prayer of "the two" will accomplish much!

People in hardships, in crisis, need our support. Sometimes fellow church members may find themselves in legal trouble. At their appointment before a judge for a verdict or sentencing, they want a pastor or a friend or a person from the church to be with them, to stand beside them. There is comfort there and power too.

God's heart is moved when He sees His children stand side by side, beckoning His mercy and His favor. To enter before the throne room of God can be overwhelming to some. A person is emboldened when they have another to go with them before the throne.

And it means something to a decision maker to see the person before him is loved enough that two or more would come before him on that person's behalf.

Coming before His throne on someone else's behalf, taking the time to yearn, to plead, to approach the Father for another, demonstrates love that the Father wants to see in His children.

When others join us in prayer, a certain filter is enacted. When we ask another to pray with us for something, a validity test is established for that prayer. If a friend wants a new Corvette and asks you to pray with him for it, you will probably politely decline. There has to be agreement between two believers that the prayer is a valid request that will glorify God and enable the requestor to do His will.

Asking others to join us in prayer is cloaked in an element of necessity; we've tried everything else. In our desperation, we open up, confess our need to another, and ask them to join us before the Father and help us move heaven to respond to our need.

Sharing a personal struggle or a private sin with another believer can be a cleansing experience. It's a greater degree of humility and contrition that blesses the heart of God.

Agreeing in prayer may allow reconciliation between two people. Sometimes a person may have a broken relationship with a brother or sister in Christ. Nothing heals division more than serious need. It's amazing how a crisis can bring people together who would not normally be in fellowship. They may have never otherwise reconciled, but because of the crisis, past offenses are talked about, forgiven, and put behind so they can move forward and deal with the issue faced before the Father's throne. We need to confess *to* each other before we pray *with* each other.

> *Therefore, confess your sins to one another and pray for one another, so that you may be healed. The urgent request of a righteous person is very powerful in its effect. (James 5:16)*

And we may not have received what we've been praying for because we haven't really believed, but then we bring someone into the equation who may be a person of great faith. When that person joins us, he not only encourages us and agrees with us that God will do it but has the faith that moves the hand of God.

Make it a part of your prayer life to regularly pray with another or others. You will be greatly blessed and so will the Lord, . . . and you know what happens then.

CHAPTER 18

PRAYING FOR HEALING

I'll be the first to admit, this one's a toughy. There's probably more that we don't know about divine healing than we do.

So let's tackle this big boy and see if God can shed some light on a very complex but important issue.

Ready for some more surprises?

- Did you know the young guys today get it right after all? Jesus and the rabbis taught sitting down.
- Did you know your relationship to your possessions is the number two theme of the New Testament, second only to salvation?
- Did you know more is said in the New Testament about Christ's second coming than His first?

So now that I have your attention about the possibility of some new truths, let's look at a few things that might surprise you about healing.

Healing is not in the atonement. Jesus healed multitudes long before He died for their sins. Jesus died for our sins not for our sicknesses. The *cross* provides redemption from the penalty of our sins. It is a different doctrine; *rapture and resurrection,* that provides for the redemption and glorification of our bodies.

Those who teach the possibility of perfect health, perfect government, or perfect environment being possible *now* are confused about their priorities and off in their timetable. The question is not *whether* He heals but *when.*

Peter says we have been redeemed. *"You were not redeemed with corruptible things, like silver or gold . . . but with the precious blood of Christ"* (1 Pet. 1:18–19 NKJV).

Paul says we are yet to be redeemed. *"Not only that, but we also who have the firstfruits of the Spirit, even we ourselves groan within ourselves, **eagerly waiting for the adoption, the redemption of our body"** (Rom. 8:23 NKJV, emphasis added).

Redemption of the soul is *here and now*; redemption of the body is close but *not yet.* Our soul *was* redeemed at our justification. Our body *will be* redeemed at our glorification.

When people say, "Healing is in the atonement," they mean that on the same basis of Christ's death on the cross by which you can claim instant forgiveness of sin, the believer can always claim instant healing from sickness. Solid biblical exposition reveals this to be incorrect.

Isaiah 53:5 (KJV) is often used as a proof-text for healing in the atonement: *"But he was wounded for our transgressions; he was bruised for our iniquities: the chastisement of our peace was upon him; and with his stripes we are healed."*

After years of research, I have not found one classical theologian, one historic Bible scholar or commentator who does not agree that, in context, the reference to healing refers to *spiritual healing from sin, not physical healing of the body.*

> *He was despised and rejected by men, a man of suffering who knew what sickness was. He was like someone people turned away from; He was despised, and we didn't value Him. Yet He Himself bore our sicknesses, and He carried our pains; but we in turn regarded Him stricken, struck down by God, and afflicted. But He was pierced because of our transgressions, crushed because of our iniquities; punishment for our peace was on Him, and we are healed by His wounds. We all went astray like sheep; we all have turned to our own way; and the Lord has punished Him for the iniquity of us all. (Isa. 53:3–6)*

There is no discussion of the healing of the body in Isaiah 53. *It portrays Israel as sick with sin and in need of healing.*

To attempt to read physical healing into this obvious context of salvation from the spiritual sickness of sin is a transgression of every time-honored hermeneutical principle.

The first chapter of Isaiah *clearly establishes* that a sick body will be used as a *metaphor* for Israel's sin throughout the entire book. Once that is established, it *never changes.*

> *Oh sinful nation, people weighed down with iniquity, brood of evildoers, depraved children! They have abandoned the LORD; they have despised the Holy One of Israel; they have turned their backs on Him. Why do you want more beatings? Why do you keep on rebelling? The whole head is hurt, and the whole heart is sick. From the sole of the foot even to the head, no spot is uninjured—wounds, welts, and festering sores not cleansed, bandaged, or soothed with oil.* (Isa. 1:4–6)

Spiritual healing from sin in Isaiah chapter 1 *does not* become physical healing from disease in chapter 53.

Paul's letter to the Romans is the classic work on the nature and purpose of Christ's atoning work on the cross.

It is of great significance to note that not a word about physical healing occurs in Romans. Surely, if it were as important a part of the theology of redemption as some suggest, Paul would have at least mentioned it in his great treatise on the subject.

Healing is according to God's timetable, not ours. Hebrews 11 is the honor roll of the greatest men and women of God who ever lived.

Verses 31–35 recount their awesome deliverance from everything imaginable—even death—all by faith:

> *By faith Rahab the prostitute received the spies in peace and didn't perish with those who disobeyed. And what more can I say? Time is too short for me to tell about Gideon, Barak, Samson, Jephthah, David, Samuel, and the prophets, who by faith conquered kingdoms, administered justice, obtained promises, shut the mouths of lions, quenched the raging of fire, escaped the edge of the sword, gained strength after being weak, became mighty in battle, and put foreign armies to flight. Women received their dead—they were raised to life again. Some men were tortured, not*

accepting release, so that they might gain a better resurrection.

Verses 36–39 recount *others equally faithful and equally hurting who received no promised deliverance at all:*

> *And others experienced mockings and scourgings, as well as bonds and imprisonment. They were stoned, they were sawed in two, they died by the sword, they wandered about in sheepskins, in goatskins, destitute, afflicted, and mistreated. The world was not worthy of them. They wandered in deserts and on mountains, hiding in caves and holes in the ground. All these were approved through their faith, but they did not receive what was promised.*

No divine rescue. Not yet that is. Not that they lived to see.

Verse 40 says, **"Since God had provided something better for us,** *so that they would not be made perfect without us"* (emphasis added).

The promised salvation of Messiah, for which they looked, was *perfected*, fulfilled, completed, experienced, in us. We look back and see that what they did not live to see happen—did happen—was perfected—whether they lived to see it or not.

With us it's *now* or *later*. With God it's always right now. God created time and will not be limited by His own creation. With Him it's always *today*. Always *right now*. Ask God why He didn't do something sooner, and He'll probably say, "Sooner than what?" With Him there is no sooner or later.

Ultimately everyone, who puts their faith in Jesus Christ as Lord and Savior will be permanently and perfectly healed with a new glorified body.

Whether living or dead, we shall be translated and conformed into His image at the rapture.

> *For this we say unto you by the word of the Lord, that we which are alive and remain unto the coming of the Lord shall not prevent them which are asleep. For the Lord himself shall descend from heaven with a shout, with the voice of the archangel, and with the trump of God: and the dead in Christ shall rise first: Then we which are alive and remain shall be caught up together with them in the clouds, to meet the Lord in the air: and so shall we ever be with the Lord. (1 Thess. 4:15–17 KJV)*

> *Behold, I shew you a mystery; We shall not all sleep, but we shall all be changed, In a moment, in the twinkling of an eye, at the*

last trump: for the trumpet shall sound, and the dead shall be raised incorruptible, and we shall be changed. For this corruptible must put on incorruption, and this mortal must put on immortality. (1 Cor. 15:51–53 KJV)

For our conversation is in heaven; from whence also we look for the Saviour, the Lord Jesus Christ: Who shall change our vile body, that it may be fashioned like unto his glorious body, according to the working whereby he is able even to subdue all things unto himself. (Phil. 3:20–21 KJV)

If all the people who have ever lived had not died from something, the world would be so overpopulated life would have ceased to exist centuries ago. Man that is born of woman is, indeed, full of trouble and of few days. The death of the body and the sickness, which precedes it, knows no final release until the rapture. In the meantime, we do, indeed, buy our glasses and take our prescriptions.

Our God heals today. Sometimes He heals through diet and health, sometimes through medicine, sometimes through prayer, and sometimes through the awaiting the glorified body. But He does heal. Our loving God answers the prayers of His children.

Healing, as all things, is subject to God's greater purpose. Paul suffered from a thorn in the flesh. It was likely a facial disfiguration, a speech impediment, or limited eyesight. Possibly all the above. His prayer for personal healing wasn't answered. God said, "My grace is sufficient for thee."

The *grace* he learned with the nonhealing of the thorn would become the theme of the great Pauline Epistles. Which was the greater purpose? Paul's healing or Paul's epistles?

Paul did not heal Timothy. He told him to drink a little wine medicinally for his stomach ailment and other chronic sicknesses. Was it the steadfast faith and spiritual grit Timothy developed in bearing the pain of his nonhealing that matured his faith to the level that, as tradition says, he could endure being stoned to death by a mob in Ephesus for his stand against the great goddess Diana at the crossroads of world paganism?

No longer able to travel due to his illness, in AD 65 Paul left a physically impaired Trophimus at Miletum—*sick*. Is it not likely, as historic tradition suggests, that he planted or helped to plant Revelation's great seven churches of Revelation from there?

Jesus prayed in the garden, "If it be Thy will, if there's any other way, let this cup pass from Me. Nevertheless, not My will but Thine be done." It wasn't. And it didn't.

God's greater purpose was to save the world.

Sometimes God answers a greater prayer by not answering a lesser one.

- Mom's greater prayer: "Lord, keep my little girl safe today."
- Mom's lesser prayer: "Lord, please let my little girl not be late for the school bus again today."
- God, "Sorry, no can do. The bus is going to crash."

John Lapos's mother prayed for her son to be birthed whole. He was born with a serious crippling malady and has always walked with a great limp. Years later, he would stand before the International Mission Board and become their first missionary approved for service with a major physical impairment. His unparalleled passion for Christ overwhelmed the board and completely negated the impact of the impairment. He became their first underground missionary in China and now serves openly in Thailand.

The relationship of the impairment to his passion established a new precedent for sending missionaries.

- My greater prayer: "Lord, let me get to Tulsa today to spend some time with my family."
- My lesser prayer: "Lord, don't let me miss the flight from Los Angeles to Tulsa."
- God, "Sorry, no can do. The plane's going to crash."
- True story.

Healing is not always what you think. Let's take a fresh look at James's frequently misunderstood teaching on prayer for healing.

> *Is anyone among you suffering? Let him pray. Is any cheerful? Let him sing psalms. Is anyone among you sick? Let him call for the elders of the church, and let them pray over him, anointing him with oil in the name of the Lord. And the prayer of faith will save the sick, and the Lord will raise him up. And if he has committed sins, he will be forgiven. Confess your trespasses to one another, and pray for one another, that you may be healed. The effective, fervent prayer of a righteous man avails much.* (James 5:13–16 NKJV)

The Jews believed that somehow sickness and suffering were always related to sin. Job was written in part to say such is not the case. Yet to this very day, the idea prevails. We remember only too well the question of the Pharisees to Jesus. *"Who sinned, this boy or his parents, that he was born blind?"*

It is explicit in James's text that some sickness is, indeed, the result of sin, and some is not. Jesus, for example, when healing the paralytic lowered through the roof by his friends, *first* forgave his sins. Other times He healed people's congenital diseases *without* dealing with their sin.

Keep clearly in focus that some sickness is related to sin and some is not. In the case where sin is the cause, sin must first be confessed and forsaken in order that the resultant disease might be remitted.

A study of the Greek text in James's passage indicates he is dealing with two kinds of sickness. In verse 13 he says, *"Is any among you afflicted?"* The Greek word for "afflicted" is *kakopatheo*, meaning "evil or bad," and *patheo*, meaning "to suffer," from which we get *pathology*. In verse 14 he simply says, "Are there any sick?" His word for "sick" is *astheneo*, meaning "under the weather for any reason."

Moral possibility is not suggested in this word *astheneo* translated "sick," though it is in the first word translated "afflicted."

James, therefore, is obviously dealing with two kinds of sicknesses. The man who is sick without any morally related absolute may call for the church to pray. And, if he, incidentally, has committed sins, they will be forgiven.

But that man who has been afflicted with *kakopatheo*—that is, pathologically ill—related to his moral transgression, is to pray for himself.

If healing is in the atonement—and all the classical theologians agree that *it is not*—if you take an aspirin for a headache, wear eyeglasses or hearing aids, get a flu shot, or put lotion on a sunburn, let alone rush to the emergency room when your child is injured in an accident, and you say you believe healing is provided in the atonement, you *insult the cross* and your actions are an affront to Calvary.

If any physical healing of the body is in the atoning work of Christ on the cross, then it is all to be found there.

The cross provides healing from all *sin*. If in this life it also provides healing for physical maladies, it provides for *all* of them or *none* of them.

God heals in many ways:

- *God heals in answer to prayer.*
- *Sometimes God heals for no apparent reason at all.* One of our twin grandsons, Harper, developed a major rash around his mouth and cheeks. No special prescriptions were applied. No special prayers offered. After a few months, it just went away.

- *God heals through the healing hands of physicians and medicine.* Some of my best friends are doctors. They are one of God's great gifts to mankind. For centuries the church has affectionately referred to Jesus as the Great Physician. Luke was called the Beloved Physician.

- *God heals through the immune system.* Medical science tells us all human beings have virtually all diseases, including cancer, in their body all the time. With a strong, healthy immune system, they are held at bay and simply never present.

- *God heals naturally.* Natural healing—also called alternative medicine, nutritional healing, holistic and homeopathic—is huge. And it's effective. It simply means "no junk, just the good stuff."

- Eat in such a way as to fortify the immune system and strengthen it to kill or suppress the toxins that make us sick. Eat everything as close to the way God made it as possible: naturally, organically, no chemicals, no food colorings, no preservatives, no pesticides, etc. Lots of natural vitamins, lots of raw food, and lots of organic fresh squeezed fruit and vegetable juices, whole grains, not bleached, etc.

- I know. We've experienced it. Two of our closest friends have fully recovered from terminal diagnoses of both Crohn's disease and cancer. Naturally. The homeopathic doctors I know are not quacks and nuts. They are PhDs and MDs.

- *God heals ultimately in the glorification of our earthly bodies,* like unto His glorious body, for we shall be like Him when we see Him as He is.

Hear my heart. I believe in divine healing. New Testament people believed in Him because they saw the miracles. I've seen the miracles because I believe in Him.

God heals. The Bible affirms it. I've seen it.

There are forty references to leprosy in the Old Testament alone—the worst disease known to man, totally incurable, fully terminal. It is the often-used biblical picture of the hopelessness of sin, except for the healing power of Christ. No physician or medical procedure has ever cured one leper in the history of mankind.

I preached a citywide evangelistic campaign in Hyderabad, India, and, to my surprise upon my arrival, learned that it had been advertised as a healing campaign. Each night I preached the gospel and prayed for the sick. Countless numbers of the thirty-five thousand nightly attenders were saved and many others healed.

One night after I prayed, Deacon Roger Bridgewater brought a man to me. "Pastor," he said, "when we prayed, I saw this man's leprosy disappear before my very eyes." His skin was as soft and pink as a newborn baby. What man had not done in centuries, God did in an instant.

America's foremost evangelist between Billy Sunday and Billy Graham was Hyman Appleman, a Russian-born, Hebrew Christian. Uldine and I with our young daughter Melodye Jan traveled with him for three years.

One Saturday afternoon, Dr. Appleman and I met in his hotel room for prayer. When I told him of Melodye's three-day long struggle with a 104-degree fever, he passionately pled with the Lord and seemed to settle into a sense of peaceful assurance that his prayer had been answered. A minute or two later, Uldine called our room. "Honey, just a minute ago," she said, "Melodye's temperature dropped to 98.6 degrees." What man could not do in three days, God did in three seconds.

Jerrye and James Taylor joined our church from my parents' church in Oklahoma where they had served on staff. Sadly, Jerrye had developed large carbuncles, hard knots on both hands and, after many medical procedures, was unable to move even a single finger. One Sunday after church Associate Pastor Harvey Kneisel and I joined the Taylors in our prayer room for a time of anointing with oil and prayer for Jerrye. When we finished, "In Jesus' name, Amen," the growths had completely disappeared, and each finger functioned normally. What man could not do over several years, God did in a second.

Thirty years later our daughter Melodye, now a wife and mother, had a second special answer to prayer.

A CAT scan revealed a large tumor at the base of her spine with fingers extending throughout her body. Suffering through months of procedures and medication, she only grew worse. Our church sincerely prayed for weeks as did her own church where her husband, Curt, served as pastor. Dr. David Wilkerson scheduled surgery.

She was prepped and the surgical team in place, but Dr. Wilkerson sensed a check in his spirit and said, "Melodye, I'm going to take one more CAT scan to make sure I saw what I saw."

Shortly he returned with the radiologist. She expected the worst. God gave her the best. "Melodye," he said, "there's absolutely nothing there; God has healed you."

One Sunday, about two hundred persons knelt at our altar as the church joined me in praying for their healing. A young college student from Uldine's Bible class knelt beside her legally blind mother. When we said, "Amen," she stood up and began to shout, "Praise God I can see, I can see!"

God heals, and He is indeed the same yesterday, today and forever. Yet many questions remain.

- Matthew 12:15 says Jesus healed them *all.* Mark 1:34 says *many* were healed. Does Mark infer that some were not?
- Jesus healed Peter's mother-in-law. Were there other family members of the disciples whom He did not heal? And if so, why were they not recorded?
- Jesus raised only Lazarus from the dead. Why not the whole graveyard?

These can remain questions without answers, for God's ways are past finding out. *"Oh, the depth of the riches both of the wisdom and the knowledge of God! How unsearchable His judgments and untraceable His ways!"* (Rom. 11:33).

God is not willing that any should perish. Yet they do. God is not willing that men murder and rape. Yet they do. Is not God unwilling that any be sick? Yet they are.

The fallen world in which we live is the result of our bad choices, not God's. And an imperfect world has imperfect people with bodily imperfections called diseases. God's perfect will is not always done in an imperfect world.

Sin, disease, suffering, death, and hell were never in God's perfect will. God could have made us like the animals with knowledge, emotion, and instinct but no moral will. But He loved us so much, He made us in His image and gave us a will to choose to love and follow Him or choose not to. We, not God, perverted that blessing. We chose to sin against Him, and we created the fallen world in which we live and of which disease is a part.

Once in heaven His will was perfectly done. In Paradise regained, it will again be done. But now we live in an imperfect world between two perfect worlds: Paradise lost.

Sometimes His answer is, "Yes." Sometimes, "No." Sometimes, "Wait awhile."

We'll never have all the answers until at last in heaven, we shall *know as we are known*. And after all the scholars have done their best, after all the theologians have come and gone, our sweet God will still be a sovereign God whose ways are sometimes past finding out and whose love never fails.

Rest in Romans 8:28.

So, how do you pray for the sick?

- With your heart. *"Let us lift up our hearts and our hands to God in heaven"* (Lam. 3:41).
- With your whole heart. *"You will seek Me and find Me when you search for Me with all your heart"* (Jer. 29:13).
- With a true heart. *"As for you, if you redirect your heart and lift up your hands to Him in prayer"* (Job 11:13).

- With a pure heart. *"The pure in heart are blessed, for they will see God"* (Matt. 5:8).
- With a fixed heart. *"My heart is confident, God, my heart is confident. I will sing; I will sing praises"* (Ps. 57:7).
- With a happy heart. *"Speaking to one another in psalms, hymns, and spiritual songs, singing and making music from your heart to the Lord"* (Eph. 5:19).

At the Pool of Bethesda, a great multitude was waiting to be healed. Jesus healed only one of them.

Later debating the issue with the Pharisees, He said He would heal people *as He chooses*. *"By the Sheep Gate in Jerusalem there is a pool, called Bethesda in Hebrew, which has five colonnades. Within these lay a large number of the sick—blind, lame, and paralyzed—waiting for the moving of the water"* (John 5:2–3).

> *And just as the Father raises the dead and gives them life, so the Son also gives life to **anyone He wants to**. (John 5:21, emphasis added)*

Just love Him. Just trust Him and let Him be God. God's pretty good at being God.

CHAPTER 19

YES . . . BUT NOT YET

Jesus taught us to see the big picture—Everything against the backdrop of His power, His provision, His priorities, His Kingdom, yes, and His timing. And only He can comprehend it all.

Time, space, circumstances, the seen, the unseen.

Always in harmony.

Always on time.

Always *on* purpose and *in* His purpose.

With Him it's never yesterday or tomorrow, it's always right now. No panic. No problem. Just peace. Just purpose.

As with the saints of Hebrews 11 and 12, every promise shall be fulfilled, every prayer prayed in faith and in His will answered, whether we live to see them or not. And so as sons and daughters of a faithful Father, we sometimes pray our prayers in the uncertain valley of "Yes . . . but not yet."

But we must and can do so in peace and in faith. It takes a bit of time for a piece of coal to become a beautiful diamond. God has given us so much to make the journey in confidence and composure. He is always faithful. He always comes through. He always answers prayers of faith and in His will, *in His time.*

Though from earthly perspective it may not *seem* so, we know that from His perfect perspective it *is* so.

The valley of the shadow of death was a precarious maze of treacherous trails through which the shepherds fatalistically ran their sheep, hurrying to "get it over with" to find the still water and green grass on the floor of the valley.

David spoke volumes when he said, "I run neither fatalistically nor in denial through the valley. I *walk* peacefully, for my Shepherd *knows* the way and *holds* my hand" (author's paraphrase).

When you have to wait, focus on the times He has come through before.

Ten of the spies on the borders of the Promised Land disbelieved God and joined the grumbling multitudes who moaned, "Oh that we had died back in the wilderness."

And God said, "Why can't they believe Me *just one more time, seeing all the things I've done for them in the past?*"

Wait. And remember, *"No temptation has overtaken you except what is common to humanity. God is faithful, and He will not allow you to be tempted beyond what you are able, but with the temptation He will also provide a way of escape so that you are able to bear it"* (1 Cor. 10:13).

Even the trial of delayed answer to prayer comes with the provision of grace. A *"way of escape"* doesn't mean no valley of despair. It means *"victory through the middle of the valley."*

The promise is not that we will not *walk* through the valley; it is that we will walk *through* the valley. We shall not die in the valley. We will come out on the other side. We shall soon live in victory where the valley ends and happily the mountains begin again.

And as you walk, remember the purpose of the delay has clearly been revealed.

> *We know that all things work together for the good of those who love God: those who are called according to His purpose. For those He foreknew He also predestined to be **conformed to the image of His Son,** so that He would be the firstborn among many brothers. (Rom. 8:28–29, emphasis added)*

God loves Jesus so much, He wants to fill up heaven with millions of sons and daughters just like Him on whom to lavish His love. We are made in the image of sinful Adam. Through the hammer and chisel of trials (even the trial of waiting), He is building a beautiful faith and patience within us that remakes us into the image of His Son.

As you wait, focus more on *who* He is than *what* He is currently doing. Let neither your faith nor your passion rise and fall on His ways but on His wonderful self.

And never forget the difference in the *acts* of God and the *ways* of God. It was an *act* of God to send fiery serpents among the children of Israel. It was the *way* of God to teach them to trust Him with their lives.

It was an *act* of God to put a lonely old man on the island of Patmos. It was the *way* of God to bring about the book of Revelation.

It was an *act of* God to lead His Son to an old rugged cross. It was the *way* of God to bring about the redemption of the world.

Don't live under the illusion that God intends for you a life devoid of problem and pain. He is a God of "Greater Purpose."

He's never in a hurry, and He never delays without purpose.

He will do what He promises, and you will be glad you waited—and waited—and waited.

I have never seen God delay to answer prayer except to answer it later in a greater way.

The last thing righteous Joseph prayed for was a fiancée impregnated by another.

God's answer, "Wait just a little bit longer—how about the virgin mother of the Savior of the world?"

And imagine Paul's disappointment in God's denial to be the apostle to a very small religious sect, "the Jews."

God's answer, "Got a little bigger plan, Paul—how 'bout an apostle to the whole world?"

Dr. Fred Minton made a three-day business trip from Dallas to San Francisco. Before he left, he put about a handful of sticky tab notes around the house for Marlane. Each with one brief message, "I love you." He was surprised when he called home that night and she said nothing about the notes. Nor the second night, nor the third. Nor at the airport when she welcomed him home on the fourth day.

The next morning he found every note still in place. Each with one added word . . . "too."

CONCLUSION

A FINAL WORD

I wrote my first book, *Young Man with a Horn*, at age twenty-four. It was the testimony of my conversion from playing jazz in clubs to serving Jesus in churches. Guess it seems a little goofy to write your life story at twenty-four, but then what can I say?

My next book, *The Power of Positive Praying*, came six years later at age thirty.

Looking back, what seems only a few weeks later, it's been a blast. Preacher—professor—evangelist—fundraiser—mentor—author—pastor.

And I've even found that God has a sense of humor. Over the last two years He used an eighty-year-old retired pastor to speak to sixteen thousand young pastors.

But my deepest satisfaction is that God has given me a shepherd's heart. I truly do care about people. Famous people and unknown. Winners and losers. Red and yellow, black and white, they are precious in His sight. And in mine.

The new *Power of Positive Praying* is filled with words such as *praise, love, joy, thankfulness, healing,* and *answered prayer.* But I know only too well that to some they are just that—only words. Words without experience, words without reality.

To some who read my first *Power of Positive Praying* and it just didn't work, let me say life changes us. Life makes us different people than we were ten years ago, or twenty, and certainly fifty. I've learned a bit, as have you.

May this new book, as you read again, be a new day for you. With all my heart, I pray this time it will be a "game changer."

The *last* thing I want to do is sell books. The *first* thing I want to do is help people. I truly pray the new *Power of Positive Praying* will bless and strengthen your life with joy and victory.

See you at the throne. The Shepherd loves the sheep.

Bro. John

NOTES

1. Andrew Murray, *Waiting on God* (Fort Washington, PA: Christian Literature Crusade, 1968, 1972).

2. Mark Batterson, *The Circle Maker* (Grand Rapids, MI: Zondervan, 2013).

3. Ronnie Floyd, *The Power of Prayer and Fasting, Revised and Expanded* (Nashville: B&H Publishing Group, 2010), 123.

Thank you God for your gift to me in beginning the month of my birthday to teach me about prayer.

I'm excited to sit at your feet daily, drink from your cup and hear from you.

You are the lover of my soul and I want to be consumed by you, I want to thirst for you.

In Jesus name I pray, amen